AGATHA CHRISTIE
AT HOME

Godfrey Argent

Hilary Macaskill

AGATHA CHRISTIE
AT HOME

F

FRANCES LINCOLN LIMITED
PUBLISHERS

Frances Lincoln Limited
4 Torriano Mews
Torriano Avenue
London NW5 2RZ
www.franceslincoln.com

PAGE 1 and RIGHT
The River Dart.
PREVIOUS PAGE
Agatha Christie at home in 1969.

CONTENTS

FOREWORD BY MATHEW PRICHARD

Agatha Christie, my grandmother, loved Devonshire. She had connections with it all her life; she was born in Torquay, and spent summers at Greenway on the river Dart right up to the year she died in 1976. In between, she spent a good portion of her leisure time there and I always found that it was at Greenway she was at her most relaxed. My grandmother was something of a collector where homes were concerned, but Ashfield in Torquay, where she was born, and Greenway always held a special place in her heart.

I think there are two important contributions (very different from each other) that Devon made to Agatha Christie's life. The first is that it was the place where she first learnt to write. Some completely unmemorable romantic stories emerged and then she hit upon the idea of the detective story and, I believe I am right in saying, she very typically went off to Dartmoor to finish *The Mysterious Affair at Styles*, the first appearance of Hercule Poirot, and there a career was born. Devon had its fair share of appearances in her later books, as Hilary Macaskill will tell you, but it is worth remembering that here was where it all started.

Later on, when I knew her best, she came to Devon in the summer to reward herself for a job (the annual Christie for Christmas) well done. Now that the book was finished, she could sit in her boathouse with her grandson and watch the tourist boats go by; she could enjoy picnics on Dartmoor; she could swim in the sea or even occasionally in the river Dart; she could eat lashings of Devonshire cream! All these pleasures you will see and enjoy with Hilary Macaskill.

Backgrounds and surroundings were very important to Agatha Christie. She used others – the English village, the Middle East, etc. – but Devon keeps recurring and this book will I hope transmit some of the magic that my whole family felt when we were there. As I write, Greenway, which is now owned by the National Trust, has just been reopened. I was almost overcome by nostalgia and I felt the same leafing through Hilary's book. I hope you enjoy it.

Mathew Prichard

Agatha Christie on the steps of Greenway with her dog Treacle. Her grandson, Mathew Prichard, can be seen behind the door.

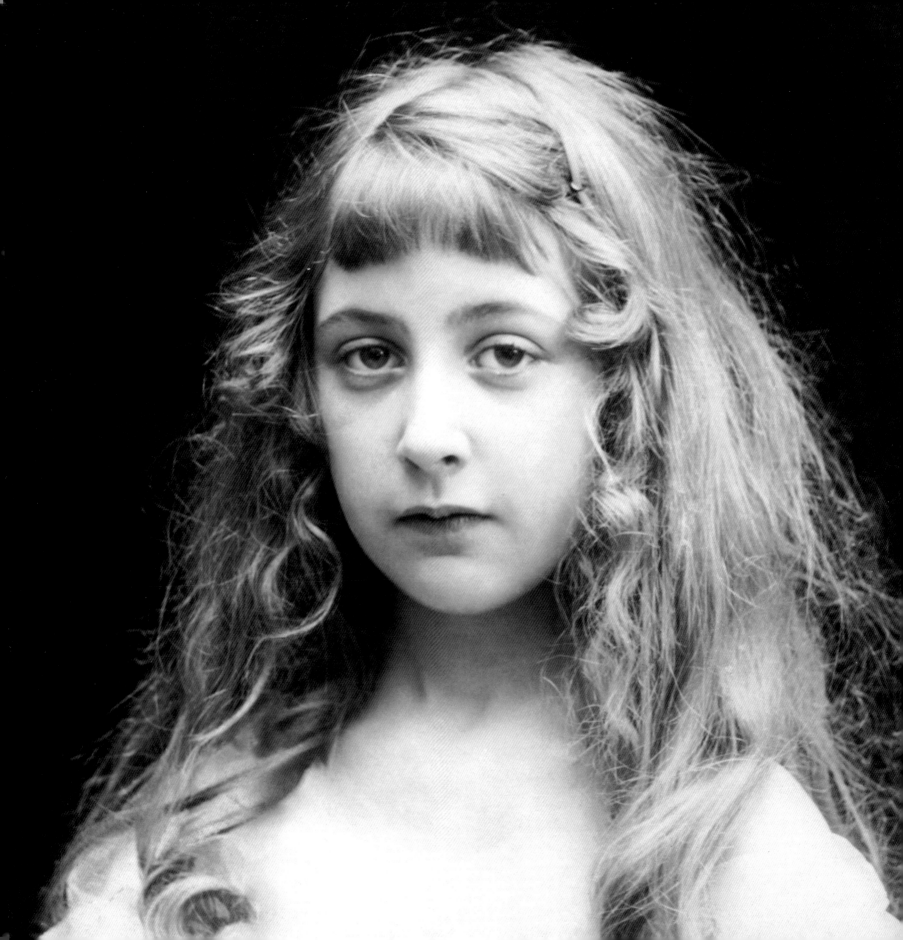

THE AUTHOR –
AGATHA MILLER-CHRISTIE-MALLOWAN

O! ma chère maison; mon nid, mon gîte,
Le passé l'habite . . . O ma chère maison

'My dear home, my nest, my house': the words from a 1958 song by Jules Bruyères, with which Agatha Christie, best-selling author of all time, opened her autobiography, sum up the importance of home to her. The homes that spanned her life – from Ashfield, her birthplace in Torquay ('a happy house'), to Greenway, on the River Dart ('a dream house') – provided the 'memories and the realities that are the bedrock' of her being and her craft. They – and the other houses she owned or knew well, along with the towns and villages of her home county – supplied plots and backdrops for her stories. Greenway, now owned by the National Trust and opened to the public in 2009, became the repository of her life and the place in her beloved Devon where she could retreat from the pressures of fame, where she loved to stay until almost the end. By visiting Greenway, one can gain an insight into the background that made her the crime writer she was. But it was at Ashfield where her creative life began.

The first stirrings of Agatha Christie's imagination, as she recounts in her autobiography, published after her death in 1977, were in the gardens of her home at Ashfield in Torquay.

Agatha Miller as a child.

These were for her a place of enchantment, of lawns and woods, of secret corners and hideaways, with infinite possibilities for make-believe. The daydreams and dramas she acted out here laid the foundations for the extraordinary storyteller that she would become. The house too was precious, and provided opportunities for pretend housekeeping that anticipated a lifetime enthusiasm for interior décor and design – and for acquiring houses. Ashfield was to remain powerfully with her for the rest of her life, and though she lived in many different houses – from mews cottage to mud-brick hut, modernist flat to mansion – the shadows of Ashfield stayed with her wherever she went.

Agatha Clarissa Miller was born on 15 September 1890, the daughter of Frederick Alvah Miller and Clarissa (always known as Clara) Miller. Agatha was their third child, but her sister Madge and brother Monty were so much older (eleven and ten years) that she was to a great extent like an only child. As Madge and Monty were away at school, she learned to create her own company and to concoct her own entertainment. Her earliest memories were of making up her own companions to play with. The first lot were 'The Kittens'. She remembers the mortification she felt when her nanny, Nursie, revealed her private world to Susan, the housemaid, and her determination thenceforth to keep silence in her games and to keep her kittens to herself.

But she was not content only with playing. She taught herself to read before she was five, notwithstanding her mother's injunction that she should not read until she was eight years old, because it would be better for the eyes and the brain – a curious about-turn for a woman who had sent her first daughter to boarding school (Miss Lawrence's School at Brighton, forerunner of Roedean). Thereafter, Agatha demanded books for every birthday and Christmas. At the age of seven, she recorded in the family's Album Confessions her favourite occupation as 'reading a play' and her favourite poets as Shakespeare and Tennyson.

Her early efforts at mastering handwriting were more painful, but when her father suggested she took up arithmetic, she was happy: 'I would set to at the dining-room window seat, enjoying myself far more with figures than with the recalcitrant letters of the alphabet.' When she was promoted to a book of problems she was in her element. That she turned out to be good at solving problems as a child should be no surprise to anyone familiar with the broad range of ingenious plotting demonstrated in her novels.

Agatha did not go to school, apart from a brief period, when she was about thirteen, at Miss Guyer's Girls' School in Torquay for two days a week to study algebra and grammar, and then a short series of schools when living with her mother in Paris in her mid-teens. In a rare BBC talk given in 1955, she attributed her decision to start writing to the fact that she had no education, and was 'gloriously idle'. But she was by no means uneducated: she had a keen interest in acquiring knowledge and was a voracious reader, as well as learning to draw and to speak French during her time in Paris. While she was there she began to study singing and the piano with great diligence and considerable talent. She seriously considered a career as a professional pianist, or as an opera singer, but she did not have the self-confidence for the first, nor a strong enough voice for the second. However, she always had a piano in

Agatha as a young woman in the garden at Ashfield.

her grown-up homes and sang and played for her own – and her family's – entertainment throughout her life.

Her creativity flourished. After her sister Madge married James Watts in 1902, Agatha would often visit the Watts' family home at Abney Hall in Cheshire – a Gothic mansion immortalized in *The Secret of Chimneys*, *After the Funeral* and 'The Adventure of the Christmas Pudding' – and she recalled how she 'would strut about, muttering to myself and gesticulating' while enacting some historical romance or drama. 'It never occurred to me to write anything down.' When she did begin to write things down, it was at the suggestion of her mother when she was recovering from flu and was bored. Her mother produced an exercise book, the first few pages taken up by laundry entries but with plenty of blank pages

AGATHA CHRISTIE AT HOME

ABOVE Agatha's Steinway in the Drawing Room at Greenway. Trained as a concert pianist, she never played in public but would often play – and sing – for her family and friends.

RIGHT Agatha, centre, in her dancing class.

for Agatha to use. This set a pattern for Agatha's working methods: using secondhand exercise books and jotters is something that she did for the rest of her life, as the accumulated collection of her notebooks shows.

She started with short stories, and then moved on to a novel, *Snow in the Desert*, set in Cairo, where her mother and she had spent three months when she was seventeen, after her mother had been ill. She had difficulties with the novel, not least, she said, because she made the mistake of having a deaf heroine. Her mother suggested she took advice from Eden Philpotts, a neighbour and friend and the celebrated author of novels about Dartmoor – novels with which

Agatha was familiar, for Dartmoor was on her doorstep and a favoured place for excursions. He also wrote detective stories, sometimes under the pseudonym Harrington Hext (and was singled out by Julian Symons in his crime fiction reference work *Bloody Murder* for the ridiculous improbabilities of his plots). Little read now, he was a best-selling author of his day: one of his plays, *The Farmer's Wife*, was even adapted as a film by Alfred Hitchcock, in 1928. A reclusive man, he was at the height of his fame when Agatha approached him, but

Torquay Town Hall, which during the First World War was turned into a Red Cross Hospital, where Agatha worked as a nurse.

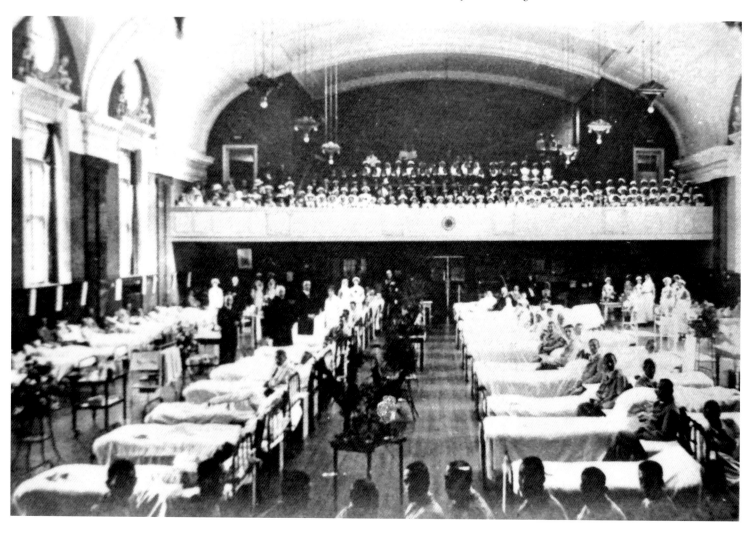

unfailingly kind and responsive, giving her encouragement, a reading list and an introduction to his agent Hughes Massie.

The turning point came while Agatha was working at the Red Cross Hospital which had been set up in Torquay Town Hall, during the First World War. She had joined the Voluntary Aid Detachment as a nurse, finding great satisfaction in the work, but later she joined her friend Eileen Morris in the newly opened

The certificate, dated 30 April 1917, from the Society of Apothecaries, which showed Agatha's qualification to work in the hospital dispensary, where she acquired her knowledge of poisons.

dispensary, where the hours were better, enabling her to help her mother look after her grandmother, who had moved into Ashfield. Together, she and Eileen mastered the intricacies of chemistry by study and experimentation – their coffee machine blew up while they were using it for Marsh's test for arsenic – and in April 1917 she received her qualifying certificate placing her on the register of assistants at the Society of Apothecaries, after having been examined in her 'skill in compounding and dispensing Medicines'.

Agatha found, however, that the work was quite monotonous, and that she had time to ponder the challenge her sister Madge, who herself wrote stories, had set her of writing a detective story. Her experience at the hospital had given her the murder weapon, and she had worked out the plot, but she needed a protagonist. Her thoughts turned to the Belgian refugees who had recently come to Torquay. Thus was born her detective Hercule Poirot, with his 'little grey cells' and obsessive behaviour. She was eventually to rather regret creating him, becoming exasperated by her small, very neat and fastidious hero. Her irritation was refracted through the prism of Ariadne Oliver, the successful detective novelist who appears in several of Agatha's novels (usually alongside Poirot) and who had become frustrated with her 'maddening' Finnish detective hero.

Halfway through writing her detective story, Agatha ground to a halt. She adjourned from Ashfield to the Moorland Hotel on Dartmoor where in a burst of activity – both mental and physical – she completed it. As she walked in the afternoons, she would act out the parts and the conversations, sleep for twelve hours and then write furiously all morning. What was also significant about this working holiday was that it developed in her a deeper affection for Dartmoor, which fed into both her life and her novels, such as *The Sittaford Mystery*, with its atmospheric setting on the edge of the moor.

She completed *The Mysterious Affair at Styles* in 1916, but it was turned down by several publishers – who must have berated themselves severely in future years – before she sent it to The Bodley

Agatha Christie conceived *The Mysterious Affair at Styles* while she was working at the dispensary at the Town Hall Red Cross Hospital in Torquay and finished it at the Moorland Hotel on Dartmoor. It was published in 1920.

Head. She heard nothing back, but she was distracted as her life reverted to normal with the ending of the war and the resumption of married life: she had married Archie Christie in 1914 when he was on leave from the Royal Flying Corps, but had barely spent any time with him since, continuing to live at Ashfield. When he was posted to the Air Ministry in London, she moved there, setting up home for the first time with great enthusiasm and demonstrating a great and enduring talent for decorating. Her daughter, Rosalind, was born in 1919. So, preoccupied with things domestic, it came as a surprise when she received a letter from John Lane of The Bodley Head agreeing to publish *The Mysterious Affair at Styles* in 1920 and offering her a meagre £25. With the blissful ignorance of a first-time author and without an agent (she had not pursued the relationship with Hughes Massie), she happily signed a contract for five books, and so began the ferociously productive routine that she kept up until the end of her life.

'The nice part about writing in those days was that I directly related it to money,' she wrote towards the end of her life. 'This stimulated my output enormously.' She would, for example, decide that she would like to remove a conservatory and fit it up as a loggia. She would get an estimate. She would plan a story. 'In due course I wrote it, and then I had my loggia.'

The Secret Adversary, Murder on the Links and *The Man in the Brown Suit* followed, as well as a number of short stories, which she wrote at the request of Bruce Ingram, editor of *The Sketch*, and which were later published as *Poirot Investigates*. But her breakthrough book was *The Murder of Roger Ackroyd* (published in 1926), the first title for her new publisher, Collins. Its plot twist caused controversy in some quarters but its ingenuity ensured that her sales increased and her reputation soared. It was, however, a traumatic year, in which her mother died, she had to sort out the family home of Ashfield and her husband demanded a divorce, all of which culminated in her disappearance for ten days. After a period of recuperation with her sister at Abney Hall, she was still deeply unhappy but, aware

AGATHA CHRISTIE AT HOME

Portrait of Agatha Christie taken by Angus McBean to mark her sixtieth birthday.

of her need to fulfil her contractual obligation, she took herself off to the Canary Islands with her daughter Rosalind and Charlotte Fisher (known as Carlo), who had been employed as governess/ secretary, to write *The Mystery of the Blue Train,* based on a short story 'The Plymouth Express' (not published in Britain until 1974 in *Poirot's Early Cases*), in which she used the familiar setting of the train she travelled in to Devon. Despite her reluctance to write the novel and subsequent dislike of it (she described it later as easily the worst book she had produced), she did complete it, demonstrating the professionalism that was to become her hallmark.

By this time, she had an agent: she had returned to Hughes Massie and met Edmund Cork, who organized the contract with Collins and was to look after her affairs for the rest of life (including dealing with her tenants, helping her with staff problems, making purchases and organizing tickets for the coronation of Queen Elizabeth). She re-embarked on her career with vigour, introducing a new detective, Miss Marple – who would soon vie in popularity with Poirot – in *The Murder at the Vicarage* (published in 1930). The following decade saw a stream of highly regarded novels.

Their creation was aided by the new stability in her life provided by her second marriage, to Max Mallowan, an archaeologist fourteen years her junior, whom she had met in 1929 at an excavation in Iraq during a trip to the Middle East. They married in September 1930, and with his encouragement and support she continued her prolific output. More importantly for her personal life, she had a husband who shared her delight in domesticity – and eating – and her interest in buying houses. Somewhat surprisingly for a woman at the time, she had started on a process of property acquisition that reached its peak just before the war, when she owned several houses in London. The most important purchase was that in 1938 of Greenway at Galmpton on the River Dart in Devon. This was the house that

Agatha with her second husband, Max Mallowan, and her dog Bingo outside Greenway House.

in the second part of her life was to be as significant to her and her family as Ashfield had been in the first. In the early years, apart from the interruptions of wartime, she and Max lived there for much of the time; later it became her cherished holiday home. In recognition of its significance, Collins issued the Greenway editions in 1966, with the cover design of three entwined fish, a symbol Agatha had spotted in an Arabian bazaar on a trip with Max.

Agatha travelled widely with Max and accompanied him on all his archaeological digs – she even had her own 'house' at Nimrud, Beit Agatha, which is where she started her autobiography in 1950 (it was completed in 1965). Her travels and her work at the digs – she was an invaluable member of the team – provided her with material for her fiction. But it was Devon, her home county, that most consistently provided inspiration and locations for her novels. Burgh Island, off the south-west coast of Devon, became Smugglers' Island in *Evil Under the Sun* and Nigger Island in *Ten Little Niggers* (later renamed *And Then There Were None*, and set on Soldier Island). Torquay, in different guises, appears in several novels, most notably in *Peril at End House*, and Greenway stars as Alderbury in *Five Little Pigs*, and as Nasse House in *Dead Man's Folly*.

She kept up an extraordinary rate of production. Along with the detective stories, mainly featuring Poirot and Miss Marple, she wrote thrillers and poetry and, under the pseudonym Mary Westmacott, six romantic novels, which dealt far more with relationships and emotions than her other books. She found a particular pleasure in writing these, and in the associated anonymity. (She was upset when her cover was blown in 1949.) Much of the material was taken straight from her life. In *Unfinished Portrait* (published in 1934), episode after episode is echoed in her autobiography. The mauve irises on Agatha's nursery wall (these recur in *Giant's Bread* too – and Miss Marple remembers them from *her* nursery in *Sleeping Murder*), the frightening Gun Man dream she used to have, the escape of Goldie the canary – and other vignettes from her life at Ashfield are transferred into that of the heroine Celia.

AGATHA CHRISTIE AT HOME

One of her most industrious years was 1940, when for much of the time she was based at Greenway, which she had bought two years earlier. She was writing two books in parallel at that time (she says in her autobiography that these were *N or M?* and *The Body in the Library,* though the second appears to have been *Evil Under the Sun:* one of her occasional slips – not so surprising in an autobiography written over fifteen years.) But there was other work too, as her correspondence with her agent shows. After dealing with her last novel, *Sad Cypress* – and expressing her rage at the cover ('I *care* about the appearance of my book') – she was, by mid-April, amending the conclusion of *One, Two, Buckle My Shoe* for the American market. She ends a letter to Edmund: 'Yours in haste and rather a bad temper as a result of fiddling with this book. I do hope they are satisfied as I want the money.'

In July, she sent Edmund *N or M?*, in which Tommy and Tuppence Beresford, who made their first appearance in *The Secret Adversary,* track down a network of spies: 'Frightfully messy, I'm afraid. Hope the typist will be able to disentangle it. As far as I can see, if the Germans invade us successfully I shall be taken straight to a concentration camp for writing this!'

Also that year Agatha began two books as insurance for Max and Rosalind, later assigning to Max the copyright of the final case for Miss Marple, *Sleeping Murder*, and to Rosalind the final case for Poirot, *Curtain*. She also wrote several short stories: mindful of the injunction from *This Week* (an American magazine which often published her fiction) against war stories – on the grounds that 'the war may be over long before we could publish' – she wrote more stories about Miss Marple. She completed two in October: 'The Case of the Retired Jeweller' and 'A Case of Buried Treasure'. In November, she finished two more: 'The Case of the Caretaker' and 'The Perfect Maid'.

Dartmoor, a favourite destination of Agatha's for excursions when she was young and later for family picnics, and used as a setting in *The Sittaford Mystery*.

THE MURDER OF ROGER ACKROYD

Agatha Christie

The Murder of Roger Ackroyd, Agatha Christie's sixth novel, published in 1926, proved to be the turning point in her writing career, as its ingenious plot secured her reputation.

So much work was she doing that she needed new typewriter ribbons: 'Do you think you could get (six) typewriter ribbons sent down to me?' she wrote to Edmund. 'Torquay has run dry of them. Black for choice and for a Portable Remington. This one is getting so pale I can hardly see it, and I am feeling rather industrious.'

Later in the war she wrote a Westmacott novel, *Absent in the Spring* – 'the one book that has satisfied me completely' – in under four days. Her writing appeared effortless, though she writes of the agony of the early weeks of creativity: 'You sit in a room, biting pencils, looking at a typewriter, walking about or casting yourself down on a sofa, feeling you want to cry your head off. Then you go out, you interrupt someone who is busy – Max usually, because he is so good-natured – and you say: "It's awful, Max, do you know I have quite forgotten how to write – I simply can't do it anymore! I shall never write another book.'

She continued her prodigious output, though not everyone entirely approved: Max's mother thought Agatha wrote so well that she should write something more serious. Agatha, whose aim was to write good detective stories, found it 'very difficult to explain to her that I was a writer for entertainment.'

In 1955, Agatha Christie Ltd was formed, in part as a response to the extraordinarily difficult state of her finances. For several years she had received no income from American sales because of tax investigations begun in 1938. (At one grim point she had to consider selling Greenway.) Then when that was all resolved, and she received the backlog of income, she was pursued by the Inland Revenue in England. The company was set up to employ Agatha and to pay her a salary to write her novels. So a new pattern emerged, in which she would write one book a year.

She had many more ideas than she could possibly ever use. The crime writer P.D. James has commented on the range of her plots: 'over and over again she came up with something that was astonishingly ingenious', but her overall approach to plotting remained something of a mystery. A.L. Rowse, the historian and Oxford academic with whom she became friendly after Max Mallowan became a Fellow of All Souls in 1962, noted that she had told him that 'in writing a detective story, you begin at the end'. But Charles Vance, who produced many of her plays, said in a magazine interview in 1990: 'She told me she created an amalgam of characters and then decided which one would die. Once she had worked that out, she then decided who had done it.'

Though Agatha credited both Lord Mountbatten and her brother-in-law, James, for providing the suggestion that led to *The Murder of Roger Ackroyd*, in general she fended off suggestions from others. One response from her agent to what amounted to a sort of begging letter, offering a number of plot-lines for money, reads: 'Mrs Mallowan has no difficulty in finding ideas for her books and prefers to use her own.' Rowse said, 'People sent plots for her to write up. She said that thinking up her plots was the one great pleasure she took in writing: all the rest was hard work.'

Inspiration could strike at any time. The Sullivans, actor friends whom Agatha often visited in Haslemere, Surrey, found her pacing round their swimming pool in deep absorption one day. When the result, *The Hollow*, was published, the dedication read: 'For Larry and Danae, with apologies for using their swimming pool as the scene of a murder.'

In the 1955 radio talk, she said, 'I do find one's friends are curious about the way one works. "What is your method?" they want to know. The disappointing truth is that I haven't much method. I type my own drafts on an ancient faithful machine I've owned for years and I find a Dictaphone useful for short stories or for recasting an act of a play . . . I think the real work is done in thinking out the development of your story, and worrying about it, until it comes right. That may take quite a while.' Once everything was in place, all that remained was 'to try to find time to write the thing. Three months seems to me quite a reasonable time to complete a book . . . On the other hand, plays I think are better written quickly.' Plays, she thought, were 'much more fun' than writing books: 'you haven't got to bother about writing long descriptions of places and people.'

Part of Agatha's pleasure in plays was in the process of production and of meeting the actors taking part: many household names made their earliest appearances in her plays – Harold Pinter, for example, appeared in several before writing his own. After seeing Joan Hickson in a small part, Miss Pierce, in *Appointment with Death* in 1946, Agatha wrote to her saying, 'I am going back to Devon on Saturday where I shall rest up and have a think. Come and have lunch with me – I will call you to play my Miss Marple one day if I can find time to write another play – too many domestic chores.' And, of course, Joan Hickson did indeed play Miss Marple, though not in Agatha's lifetime.

When she had the germ of an idea, she would, like most writers, make notes. She scrawled ideas in half-used school exercise books – an old maths jotter, a spiral-bound notebook, a red Silvine or a blue Sterling exercise book, with ruled lines. There might be a few pages of algebra, and then a list of characters, or a snatch of dialogue, or a question: 'Letters to dead. How work it in?' One book, for example, has much of the cast list of characters from *The Hollow*, followed by snatches of conversation, and a line from Poirot: 'Yes, it is always possible to put on an act.' Then she might turn the book upside down and start at the other end. In another book, after a few notes about her planned memoirs ('A chapter on parents; Ashfield – a chapter'), she embarks on a new novel, *The Clocks*. Some of her jottings are as follows:

Bit about typists in the office . . .

Miss M furious – My girls

Poirot arrives at Marine Hotel

Mildred Pebmarsh [she becomes Millicent in the final version]
   – fiftyish – blind – had been a charmer. Now teaches Braille.

Alice Dale, a young stenographer (Is her second name
   Rosemary?) . . .

Colin Lamb – young man (journalist Doctor? Investigator?)
   on vacation

In the middle there might be a note about something completely different, as when just before Mildred Pebmarsh she writes: 'Next Tuesday I have to attend a sale of authors' manuscripts.'

She was scrupulous about facts, particularly where poisons were concerned. Poison was one of her favourite methods of dispatching the victim: she used it in eighty-three stories, according to a 1978 research paper by Peter and John Gwilt ('Dame Agatha's Poisonous Pharmacopoeia' in the *Pharmaceutical Journal*), which itemizes the poisons used – from strychnine and arsenic to venom from boomslang snake – and the method of administration.

In a letter to a Dr Stephen Laing in Dorset, in 1967, she asked first about ethyl chloride ('Yes, it is an excellent instant anaesthetic,' he replied), and then about thalidomide in the birthday cake icing: 'More attractive than porridge, I think!' she wrote. 'Would the unlucky victim pass out at the tea table? Or would it be a long-term business?' With scant regard for the value of a letter from the Queen of Crime, he wrote his reply in the margin of hers and returned it to her: 'I thought it would be easier if scribbled my reply here. If it was one of those interminable Scottish teas, then the unlucky victim would certainly pass out before its end (but then who wouldn't?). Thalidomide takes about 30–40 minutes to act and a dose of three grains . . . is enough to cause 6 hours sleep at least.'

A.L. Rowse writes admiringly in his *Memories and Glimpses* of her 'first-class brain, an extraordinary combination of perception and common sense. She was extraordinarily good at sorting out problems, as all the world knows.' She, for her part, was impressed by his work. When he sent her a copy of his much-anticipated book on Shakespeare, which identified the Dark Lady of the sonnets, she wrote to him: 'Let the Lowbrow Detective salute the Highbrow Detective with appropriate humility.'

Agatha at her writing desk, which can be seen in the Drawing Room at Greenway.

Intriguingly, Rowse began to read her stories, and praised her gifts for creating character, wide understanding of human beings, natural and convincing dialogue, and firm constructions and setting of scenes: generous praise for an academic renowned for his sharp tongue. He also had a go at psychoanalysing her through her stories – for example, through the opinions of the murder victim's wife in *Five Little Pigs*, adding with a flourish: 'I don't suppose anyone has noticed that the husband's initials Amyas Crale – A C – were the same as Archie Christie.'

A.L. Rowse astutely observed the way her life fed into her work. She was 'a compulsive writer: writing was her life. Or one of her two lives – for outwardly she had a full and normal social life, family, two marriages, friends, hospitality, entertainments, housekeeping (which she was very good at), shopping (which she very much enjoyed). She had even, through Max, something of an academic circle. All ministered to Agatha's inner life of the imagination.'

Agatha Christie novels had become accepted reading in that academic circle. Geoffrey Lewis, Professor of Turkish at Oxford, recalled a conversation with Max in which he said how much he and his wife had enjoyed *The Pale Horse*. Max had looked a little embarassed and said, 'Oh dear. I suppose I had better read it then.'

As Rowse had observed, Agatha wrote about what she knew about – just like Ariadne Oliver who in *The Pale Horse* (1961) explained that she did not write about the world of Chelsea because she was afraid of getting the terms wrong: 'It's safer, I think, to stick to what you know' – such as, she added, holidaymakers on cruises and in hotels, or workers in shops and hospitals. And there was always Agatha's own life to fall back on. She resurrected Mr P., the pharmacist she so vividly describes in her autobiography who kept curare in his pocket, as Zachariah Osborne, a respectably dapper chemist in *The Pale Horse*. The *Kildonan Castle* on which she sailed to South Africa with Archie on a round-the-world working trip in 1923, reappears as the *Kilmorden Castle* bound for Cape Town in *The Man in the Brown Suit*. A letter to Max in 1931 describes in lively terms a catastrophic journey on the Orient Express when the train was stranded in the Balkans because of a flood. The journey ended two days late but the circumstances and the travellers – 'an elderly American lady, a Hungarian Minister and his wife, a large jocose Italian and a *terrible* man from Chicago' – provided source material for *Murder on the Orient Express*, which was published two years later.

Apart from Celia in *Unfinished Portrait* perhaps, who seems like Agatha in almost all respects, no one character is taken completely from life – but it is interesting to speculate which traits the author might share with her creatures. Anne Beddingfield in *The Man in the Brown Suit* (1924*)*, for example, might well have been Agatha in a parallel universe. Agatha's descriptions of her heroine as a poor sailor with plans to become a parlourmaid if need be echo Agatha's brief determination to desert ship at Madeira and make her living thus after a particularly choppy crossing of the Bay of Biscay. Emily

Trefusis, the 'quick-witted and independent-minded' heroine of *The Sittaford Mystery* (1931*)*, is another whose personality is rather in keeping with Agatha's own character.

A few years later, there is Ariadne Oliver, who has a passion for apples and notably untidy work methods – characteristics she shares with her creator. Ariadne Oliver's first appearance, in *Parker Pyne Investigates*, Agatha's twenty-second book, published in 1934, is as the authoress of forty-six successful works of fiction, all best-sellers, and with translations in French, German, Italian, Hungarian, Finnish, Japanese and Abyssinian. What must have looked liked comic exaggeration to Agatha at the time of writing turned out to be an underestimate. Some decades later, she received a letter from the novelist Daphne du Maurier from Cannes that said: 'I have the pleasure of telling you that your paperbacks were in all the bookshops, in French and in English, and much to my mortification *none* of mine. I was quite put out!'

Agatha had become friendly with many pillars of the literary establishment by this time. Poet and novelist Robert Graves became a friend when living in Galmpton in Devon during the war, and she dedicated *Towards Zero* to him in 1944.

Dear Robert,

> Since you are kind enough to say you like my stories, I venture to dedicate this book to you. All I ask is that you should sternly restrain your critical faculties (doubtless sharpened by your recent excesses in that line!) when reading it.
> This is a story for your pleasure and *not* a candidate for Mr Graves' literary pillory!

Your friend, Agatha Christie

She must have been relieved, in the circumstances, when the *Times Literary Supplement* described *Towards Zero* – an unusual book in the Christie canon, with its much greater stress on the interplay between characters – as 'masterly storytelling'.

Later, P.G. Wodehouse became a pen pal, writing an enthusiastic letter to her in 1971 in support of *Passenger to Frankfurt* (a book her family and agent were somewhat reserved about). A note he wrote inside a Christmas card a few years afterwards says: 'I often wonder how you write – I mean do you sit upright or at a desk? I ask because I find these days I can't get out of my chair and face my desk and when I write in an armchair I have the greatest difficulty in reading what I have written. This may be because I have a dachshund, a Boxer and one of our seven cats sitting on me. But oh, how I have slowed up. It's terrible.'

Agatha's reply is not known, but she did towards the end of her life move on to dictating her novels. She had tried this once before in September 1952 when she broke her wrist, which led to a suggestion from Edmund that she try out a Time Master: 'I enclose a pamphlet about it. I tried one, and it seemed quite wonderful.'

As her correspondence with her agent shows, she could be very accessible to readers too, even to the extent of inviting them to her Devon home. In 1951, for example, her agent received a letter from a teacher in Sweden ('your books are very much read over here') who was bringing a 'party of Professional Swedish ladies and gentlemen' to England in July and would like to meet her. Agatha was surprisingly receptive, writing to Edmund that he could accept on her behalf, thinking it was a good thing to do 'at the cost of one hour's misery!!'; she invited the party to Greenway and provided a buffet lunch for twenty-six.

She often asked him to reply on her behalf, but on occasion she would reply directly with vigour and humour, as to 'a former devoted Christie reader' who had said her recent books were 'as arid as a vase of sand'. 'Fortunately by the same post, I got a letter from an Air Raid warden in London who said that my book was the only thing that has taken her mind off the bombs and that she had a really good time with it. So I think the two opinions cancel out!' But she did equally agree that 'Poirot is rather insufferable. Most public men are who have lived too long. But none of them like retiring! So I'm afraid Poirot won't either – certainly not while he's my chief source of income!'

And he certainly was. Depicted on a postage stamp in Nicaragua and given an obituary in the *New York Times* when the book containing his last case, *Curtain*, was published, Poirot has a worldwide reputation. As does his creator. In 1959 UNESCO calculated that the Bible had been translated into 171 languages, Agatha Christie into 103, Shakespeare 90. Agatha Christie, author of over 100 novels, collections of short stories and plays, remains the most translated individual author in the world, and the market is ever expanding: two recent languages added are Maltese and Manx. All of these are facts about the public person, the author Agatha Christie. What is less well known is the importance of home – or homes – to the private woman.

A note on Greenway headed paper would often presage an invitation to one of the house parties Agatha was fond of holding.

THE HOUSES –
FROM DOLLS' HOUSE TO GREENWAY

*'What I liked playing with as a child, I have liked
playing with later in life. Houses, for instance.'*

Agatha Christie's interest in houses began at an early age. One of her childhood pastimes, probably as familiar to youngsters today as then, was making houses under tables, draped with bath towels 'out of which we emerged on all fours'.

In common with many children, she was given a two-storey dolls' house, with a façade that opened on to a kitchen, sitting room and hall on the ground floor, and two bedrooms and a bathroom upstairs. It was one of her proudest possessions. With her singular determination and attention to detail, she set about furnishing it, using her pocket money to buy minute dishes of food such as roast chicken and eggs and bacon, as well as small baskets of cutlery and sets of glasses. To the suite of blue satin chairs in the drawing room she added a sofa and an armchair; then she bought dressing tables with mirrors, dinner tables, dining-room suite, lamps, epergnes and bowls of flowers, along with all the usual tiny household implements for cleaning and cooking. 'Soon my dolls' house looked more like a furniture storehouse.'

Agatha's bedroom at Greenway, with its sweeping views down to the River Dart, still has the colour scheme she chose.

What happened next was slightly less universal: she asked for another dolls' house. Her mother thought this was a little excessive, and after some negotiation, a compromise was arrived at, whereby the house was placed in the playroom as an adjunct to a cupboard which – when suitably wallpapered – turned the standard dolls' house into a six-storey mansion.

Just as popular with the young property magnate was house-moving, which she would undertake once a week, using a cardboard box as the furniture van and pulling it round the playroom with a piece of string.

When recounting these early memories in her autobiography, she drew out the connections with her adult life: 'I can see quite plainly now that I have continued to play houses ever since. I have gone over innumerable houses, furnished houses, decorated houses, made structural alterations to houses. Houses! God bless houses!'

Agatha Christie's first home, Ashfield, – 'an ordinary enough villa', she called it, on the edge of Torquay in the older part, Tor Mohun – remained with her always, though she finally moved out of it in 1938. Even towards the end of her life, she dreamt of Ashfield, 'the old familiar setting where one's life first functioned'.

An ordinary villa is perhaps a relative term. What made this far from ordinary for a small child was the garden – the huge expanse of lawns, woodland and secret hiding places. It was an important playground, full of trees which each had a particular significance: the strikingly tall wellingtonia, the cedar, the big beech tree with its 'pleasant shedding of beechnuts, which I ate with relish'. Even at the end of her life she was nostalgic for the ash trees, the pines and elms and the dark ilex. Her final novel, *Postern of Fate* published in 1973, contains many features that are really recollections of the Ashfield garden, and echo the descriptions in her autobiography of the greenhouse, named KK, containing Mathilde the rocking horse and Truelove, a painted horse and cart with pedals.

The house, cluttered with precious collections made by her parents and grandmother, was equally treasured. 'How well I know every detail there: the frayed red curtain leading to the kitchen, the sunflower brass fender in the hall grate, the Turkey carpet on the stairs, the big, shabby schoolroom with its dark blue and gold embossed wallpaper,' she wrote elegaically. And in *Dumb Witness*, the precise description of Miss Emily Arundell's drawing room, which conjured up memories of the past with its faint fragrance of pot-pourri, faded rose-garlanded chintzes, prints and watercolours, sounds as though it is taken from her own memory. 'There was a good deal of china – fragile shepherds and shepherdesses. There were cushions worked in crewel stitch. There were faded photographs in handsome silver frames. There were many inlaid workboxes and tea caddies.'

At the start of her autobiography, she described how her mother, Clara Miller, came to buy Ashfield, more or less on a whim. Her parents were on holiday in Torquay, then at the peak of its popularity as a stylish and genteel resort (it introduced palm trees from New Zealand, and a byelaw stipulating that 'no person of the male sex shall at any time bathe with 50 yards of the ladies' bathing machines'). Her father was recalled on a business matter to New York, his home town and where the family was intending to settle, and charged his wife with finding a furnished house to rent while awaiting his return. Instead she bought one, using a legacy from

ABOVE Agatha's mother (left) and her grandmother in the garden at Ashfield.

RIGHT Agatha in the garden at Ashfield with her father and her first dog, Tony, short (as she recounts in her autobiography) for George Washington, the name given by her father.

her aunt's husband. According to Agatha, she saw about thirty-five houses and liked only this one. She loved the house immediately.

Ashfield worked the same magic on Agatha who, as a child a decade younger than her brother and sister, relished the solitude to exercise her imagination, which was active from the very earliest days. She had a make-believe character Mrs Green, for example, who had a hundred children, of whom 'the important ones were Poodle, Squirrel and Tree. Those three accompanied me on all my exploits in the garden.'

Agatha had a comfortable and happy childhood, the focus of her parents' attention, until she was eleven, when her father died. Her mother planned to sell the house and move somewhere smaller, but her children, and especially Agatha, persuaded her to remain at Ashfield. Even in later life when she was living in London or Berkshire, Agatha would return to Torquay for long periods to stay with her mother. Her daughter Rosalind was born there and Rosalind once said: 'Although we moved to London shortly after my birth, Ashfield seemed to be our home.' When times were hard for Agatha's mother, and Agatha and her first husband Archie

could not afford to supplement her small income, Archie suggested that Ashfield be sold, but the idea appalled Agatha. To her need to preserve Ashfield and to Archie's subsequent proposal that she write another book to make the money to do so can be attributed the making of a publishing phenomenon.

After her mother's death in 1926, Agatha used Ashfield as a base until her second marriage, and then as her summer home until she sold it in 1938. In the 1930s, she would invite friends there for the weekend, such hospitality being a prelude to the house parties she would later hold at Greenway. It was one of these occasions that,

AGATHA CHRISTIE AT HOME

LEFT Ashfield in Barton Road, Torquay, with its large gardens. Agatha knew each tree, from the monkey puzzle tree (on the left) to the firs.

RIGHT This room at Ashfield displays a part of the collections made by Agatha's family, some of which can now be seen at Greenway.

indirectly, was responsible for a revolution in publishing, Penguin paperbacks. Allen Lane, who had become firm friends with Agatha when he had met her at The Bodley Head, often visited Agatha in Torquay, trawling through bookshops and 'popping in and out of antique shops.' In *Allen Lane: a Personal Portrait*, his friend and colleague Bill Williams writes: 'His own explanation was that it all began sometime in 1934 when he was returning from a weekend in the country with Agatha Christie. While Allen waited for his train he searched the bookstall for something to read on the journey, but found nothing except expensive titles and garish reprints of rubbish. Surely, he thought (or so he used to say), there should be a demand for good, well-produced literature at a modest price.'

In recognition of her contribution to publishing history, her first novel, *The Mysterious Affair at Styles,* was included in the first set of Penguins, though because of a copyright complication it was hastily withdrawn and replaced by *Murder on the Links.* (In 1948, she was awarded the rare accolade of having a 'ten' – when ten titles of an author were published.)

Ashfield, for all its importance in her life, was essentially the home of her parents. Her own adult domestic experiences started somewhat modestly in her first home with Archie Christie at 5 Northwick Terrace, just off Maida Vale in London. The house was big, so the rooms in the flat on the second floor were spacious, and pleasantly, if shabbily, furnished. Mrs Woods, the caretaker, agreed to 'do' for the Christies, teaching Agatha details of shopping, such as how to spot an orange that had just been soaked in boiling water to make it look fresh and how to check a fish was fresh (she advised that the only way to check was to poke it in its eye, despite Agatha's concern that this seemed rather indelicate).

After the birth of their daughter Rosalind, Archie and Agatha took a short lease on another, much larger, furnished flat: four bedrooms and two sitting rooms for £5 a week in Addison Mansions, behind Olympia – two blocks of flats owned by the food company Lyons, and later demolished to make way for Cadby Hall, Lyons'

headquarters. Because that was a limited let, there was then a search for an unfurnished flat that took Agatha through Hampstead, Chiswick, Pimlico, Kensington and St John's Wood.

This flat hunt revealed something of Agatha's business acumen. She and Archie found a suitable flat in Battersea, but problems arose and it seemed they would not be able to move in at the time required; so, in desperation, they signed to buy a 'charming' little house in Scarsdale Villas, between Kensington High Street and Cromwell Road. Two days later, over breakfast, Agatha saw an advertisement for an unfurnished flat to let in Addison Mansions, virtually on the doorstep, and, though the flats were scheduled for eventual demolition, she leapt at the chance, rushing across the courtyard and charging up the stairs of the block opposite. The rather disconcerted tenant, still in her dressing gown, was a little reluctant to show her round. So, while still only on the doorstep, Agatha gasped, 'I think it will do for us. I'll take it.'

Having agreed there and then on a payment for the linoleum and fittings, she returned home triumphantly. At which point, the phone rang and the lady from Battersea said that they could move into her flat after all. As Archie pointed out, they suddenly found themselves with two flats and a house that they had agreed to buy. They disentangled themselves from the house, but instead of doing the same with the Battersea flat, Agatha hit on the idea of taking it on as well, saying to Archie that they could then ask a premium for it from someone else, which would pay for the one on the new flat. In her autobiography, she congratulated herself on this 'moment of high financial genius'. It was indeed a canny move that set the tone for her future property negotiations.

On taking possession of her new home, another skill of Agatha's came to the fore: that of interior design. It was a talent that she continued to show in later life: her second husband Max Mallowan

Agatha, always keen on the practicalities of decoration, painting the fireplace of her bedroom at Greenway.

AGATHA CHRISTIE AT HOME

Family photographs on the piano at Greenway showing four generations: Agatha second from right, with (from left) her mother Clara, grandson Mathew and daughter Rosalind.

referred in his memoirs to 'her genius for decorating houses'. Much later, when staying at Pwllywrach, Rosalind's home in Glamorgan, she wrote to Max of the longing of the 'inferior decorator' to do up Rosalind's house.

Agatha flung herself into the business of transforming the flat in Addison Mansions, not only by selecting designs and colours but also by doing some of the actual painting and wallpapering too. She was well schooled by the professional decorator they employed (though she complained that he had not told her that paint was hard to remove from the floor once it had dried). Archie decided on the décor for the bathroom – a brilliant scarlet-and-white tiled

paper – but it was Agatha who realized the concept, with the help of the professional. He showed her how to cut and fold wallpaper ready for pasting and to be bold, rather than tentative.

For Rosalind's bedroom she chose pale yellow with a frieze of paper animals – from Heal's, then as now a stylish furnishings department store – round the top. The sitting room, a small but sunny room at the back of the flat, particularly demonstrated Agatha's distinctive approach – which led to an argument with the decorator. Agatha's plan was to have very pale pink distempered walls and to paper the ceiling with a black glossy paper with hawthorn all over it. It would give her the feeling of being in the country. The professional profoundly objected, so unusual was this plan, saying that it was the wrong way round and nobody ever did it. But it was done, and he grudgingly admitted that it did look quite pretty if one looked up. Agatha was vindicated. That was the idea, she said: 'I like to think I'm under a hawthorn tree.'

Soon after they had all settled in, her first book, *The Mysterious Affair at Styles*, was accepted and with alacrity she set to work writing books and short stories. And so it was that she and Archie could afford, in 1923, to move to Sunningdale in Berkshire, which became well known later as an enclave of the rich and famous. First they lived at Scotswood, a Victorian house that had been divided into flats, with curtains of lilac, bluebells, poppies, buttercups and daisies – Agatha's fondness for flowers endured throughout her life. (The wallpaper Gwenda envisages in *Sleeping Murder* with little bunches of poppies alternating with bunches of cornflowers – an important visual detail in the plot – would very much, one feels, have met Agatha's approval.) It was not exactly the cottage in the country that she had been after, but it was nearer her beloved countryside and near Archie's beloved golf courses.

It was not long before they were on the move again. After a year or two, and having looked at many houses, something Agatha always enjoyed, they found a house in the same town – 'a sort of millionaire-style Savoy suite transferred to the country' with panelled walls, basins in the bedrooms and several bathrooms. In honour of her new career – and purchasing power – she renamed it Styles, but it turned out to be, as Agatha noted that it had been for its previous residents, an unlucky house, for it was in this house that her marriage ended.

During the turbulent period that followed, her home-making instinct came to the rescue. She bought a pretty mews cottage

The location of *Murder in the Mews*, published in 1937, may well have been inspired by Agatha's own mews home in Cresswell Place in London, which she bought in 1929.

in London at 22 Cresswell Place near the Boltons, just south of the Old Brompton Road – one of a few houses in the mews that resembled 'old-fashioned country cottages'. It is there still, its Agatha Christie plaque adjacent to the burglar alarm. She involved herself in extensive alterations, rearranging the stable and loose boxes, and making additions, including the frieze of a herbaceous border, which gave the illusion of a cottage garden, and a bathroom 'made splendid with green dolphins prancing round the wall' and matching bath.

This home was to prove life changing, when with her customary generosity she lent it to friends, an act that changed the course of her life. In the autumn of 1928, a couple of days before she was due to take a holiday in the West Indies, she went to a dinner party where two other guests, enthusing about Iraq, reawakened in her a long-held ambition to travel on the Orient Express. So she changed her plans and went instead to Baghdad, travelling on to the dig at Ur. There she met the archaeologist Leonard Woolley and his wife Katherine, her path smoothed by *The Murder of Roger Ackroyd,* which was a favourite book of Mrs Woolley's. In the summer of 1929, she invited them to stay in her London home, and there they dreamed up a plan to invite Agatha to Ur again at the end of the digging season that year and then travel on with them to Greece. It was on this trip that she met Leonard Woolley's assistant, Max Mallowan.

Though Max was fourteen years younger than her, they got along famously. When she badly sprained her ankle in Athens as she was about to return to England suddenly because Rosalind had pneumonia, he insisted on accompanying her home on the train. Not many weeks later, when he was back in London working at the British Museum, she came up from Devon on the night train to attend a publisher's party and invited him for breakfast at Cresswell Place. Her future was sealed. On 11 September 1930, after she had lived in Scotland for three weeks so that the banns could be called, they were married discreetly in Edinburgh at St Cuthbert's (as her

marriage certificate says, though in her autobiography she says it was St Columba's).

During the 1930s, Agatha indulged her enthusiasm for houses and went on a property-buying spree. Many years later, she wrote gleefully of this favourite pursuit, describing how when she and Max visited Delphi on their honeymoon, they fantasized about building a house there: she was, she said, always choosing sites for houses. Since the days of playing houses when she was a child, houses had been her passion, and at one point, not long before the Second World War, she was 'the proud owner of eight houses. I had become addicted to finding broken-down slummy houses in London and making structural alterations, decorating and furnishing them.' When, during the war, she had to pay war damage insurance on them all, she was not so happy. 'However in the end they showed a good profit when I sold them. It had been an enjoyable holiday while it lasted.'

Despite her portfolio, she often found herself having to rent when in London, having handed over her keys to friends who found themselves without accommodation, or having let to tenants. The tenants sometimes created problems, as in 1951 with Mr Portner, who leased Cresswell Place but sub-let it without permission. Another time there was a roof leak and according to a letter from Edmund Cork, who often had to deal with such details, Portner had 'instructed Harrods to repair it and is now seeking to get us to pay their bill'.

Agatha generally favoured the Kensington and Chelsea area. After she married Max, she bought 47 and 48 Campden Street – which had been turned into one house with a pleasant roof garden – because it was convenient for travel to the British Museum. She kept this until the Second World War when her secretary Carlo Fisher undertook to sell it, charging the buyers £500 more than the stated price because she was annoyed by their comments on the décor.

One home Agatha adhered to was 48 Swan Court, an apartment in a big block with an imposing arched entrance and central courtyard, which stretches from Flood Street to Chelsea Manor Street, just south of the King's Road. A neighbour was the actress Dame Sybil Thorndike, whom she came to know well. Agatha bought this after the war, and, as usual, she made it comfortable with deep pale-blue sofas and black-and-gold papier-mâché tables. Swan Court and Cresswell Place alternated as her London residence for the rest of her life.

But the London house she was attached to more than most was 58 Sheffield Terrace, off Kensington Church Street. (In her autobiography she said it was 48, but when the house was awarded a Blue Plaque in 2001, English Heritage historian Emily Cole found that her name was on the electoral register for 58.) It was a house she wanted to live in as soon as she saw it. The layout was perfect, including a room for Max's library, with space for large tables to take papers and pottery, as well as a chimney designed by him. Max had had experience of many fireplaces and chimneys in the Middle East, and turned his hand to this. Despite the gloomy prognostications of the builder, his plan worked. His chimney did not smoke and had an Assyrian brick with cuneiform writing over the mantelpiece, so the room was 'clearly labelled as an archaeologist's private den'.

Unlike the arrangements in Agatha's previous houses, the left-hand room at the top was to be her workroom and sitting room. There would be no telephone, but it would have a grand piano, a large table, a sofa, an upright chair for typing and an easy chair, and there was to be 'nothing else'. Before this, she had used corners of tables in sitting rooms, bedrooms or kitchens. (She would probably have laughed uproariously at the comparison, but Jane Austen did something similar.) She did not repeat the experiment in future houses for many decades.

The attraction of Sheffield Terrace was, as she explained, the spaciousness. There were advantages to large rooms: easier to clean, for example, than a small room 'where one's behind is always getting terribly in the way'. But the real appeal was that the feeling of space reminded her of the large rooms at Ashfield.

Lawn Road Flats, also known as the Isokon Building, was compared by Agatha to an ocean liner and where she rented a flat between 1940 and 1946.

However, it was a house that suffered in the war. She wrote to Edmund Cork in 1940 from Devon: 'Sheffield Terrace was hit a few days after we left! Front door and steps blown up – roof and chimney – windows etc but contents not much hurt owing to thick curtains and shutters. Houses next door and opposite completely flattened. So we would have had a rude awakening had we been there!' She said ruefully later, 'my Steinway was never quite the same afterwards'. Her novel *Taken at the Flood*, written in 1948, describes the bombing of a house which must have been derived from this experience.

The most unusual London home she was associated with was Lawn Road Flats, the spectacular 1934 modernist block in Hampstead commissioned by Jack Pritchard, owner of the Isokon furniture company, designed by young architect Wells Coates and described by Nikolaus Pevsner as 'giant's work of the 1930s'. It was restored in 2005. Quite unlike the chintzy comfort of Agatha's

other homes, it represented a truly modern vision with its roof terrace, central laundry and restaurant (run by the first television cook Philip Harben), and small cabin-like flats, with snugly hinged foldaway plywood tables and sliding partitions, all very ship-shape – Agatha likened the building to an ocean liner. In 1941, she and Max moved into number 17, she living in solitary comfort there through the rest of the war, while Max was working for the Air Ministry in the Middle East.

Lawn Road Flats became a rendezvous for many artists such as Henry Moore and Barbara Hepworth, and in recognition of its unique modernism, many architects and designers such as Walter Gropius and Marcel Breuer from the Bauhaus lived

The refurbished flats in the Isokon Building feature original or replicated fittings and the same sliding doors to maximize the limited space of the 'minimal' interiors.

here, as did Diana Rowntree, the *Guardian*'s first architecture correspondent, who described her love of it, saying 'it was a marvellous thing to live in the functional, light-drenched architecture'.

What Agatha loved most was the view from her window of the grassy bank with its trees and shrubs and the 'big, white, double cherry-tree which came to a great pyramidal point'. The cherry-tree cheered her every morning when she woke.

Agatha worked hard during this period: on the days when she was not working at University College Hospital dispensary – utilizing the skills she had acquired in Torquay during the First World War – she was writing. Sometimes, amid all the work and turmoil, she would, she wrote to Max, take refuge in the flat and 'lie back in that funny chair here which looks so peculiar and is really very comfortable [an example of the Isokon chair can be seen at Burgh House in Hampstead], close my eyes and say "Now where shall I go with Max?" Often it is Leptis Magna . . . or Delphi or up the mound at Nineveh.' On his fortieth birthday she wrote to him from there: 'If I had been so faint-hearted as not to marry you, I should have missed the best and happiest years of my life,' and later: 'What a lovely time we will have when we are together again – how we shall eat! Chairs covered with books and lots of laughing. – And we will talk and talk and talk.'

Her home-making skills remained in evidence throughout her life. Nigel Wollen, the family solicitor, says she loved making a home. Even when accompanying her husband on digs, which she did until the fifties, she valiantly set up home in the most difficult of circumstances, not least of which was the English requirement for afternoon tea and four-course dinners, a challenge to which she rose admirably, and always dressing for dinner. She wrote in her memoir *Come, Tell Me How You Live* (published in 1946), a light-hearted account of the archaeological way of life, of how when she returned to Chagar Bazar in 1936 she felt 'an immense wave of excitement as I catch sight of Our House. There it stands, with its dome, looking like a shrine dedicated to some venerable saint.'

She was extraordinarily resilient in the basic conditions there, but she loved the life – as she shows in this lyrical passage: 'Here some 5000 years ago was *the* busy part of the world. Here were the beginnings of civilisation and here, picked up by me, this broken fragment of a clay pot, hand-made, with a design of dots and cross-hatching in black paint, is the forerunner of the Woolworth's cup out of which this very morning I have drunk.'

The ritual of afternoon tea played a great part in Agatha's life, though what she most liked to drink was cream.

Agatha's influence meant that the quarters they lived in were sometimes a cut above the average. In Max's first independent dig in 1933 at Arpachiyah they had a house with a pretty garden filled with roses; and, as they were short of furniture, they commissioned carpenters to remedy this deficit, the pièce de resistance being the construction of pigeonholes designed for the storage of pottery – the envy of many visitors. The house had a flat roof, which came into its own as a place to spread the fragments from a potter's workshop; she wrote of a great burnished dish, 'deep red with a petalled rose centre', broken into seventy-six pieces, but each piece was still there. When it was reassembled, she was 'bursting with happiness'.

Her practical nature extended from housekeeping to cleaning artifacts – her favoured implements being an orange stick and a jar of cleansing cream. Before embarking on her Middle East trips, she had been trying to learn to draw to scale, so that she could be of assistance. But her main role eventually was as photographer. Max wrote in his memoirs, 'we were now and again banished from the living-room which Agatha had perforce to use as a dark room for developing negatives, an easy transition, for there was never much light in it! We were then forbidden to walk about upstairs, otherwise mud fell into the photographic dishes with a resounding plop.'

In 1947, they bought a house in Baghdad, an old Turkish house with a courtyard, on the banks of the Tigris. They would stay there on the way to digs, making forays to buy *kelims*, furniture and curios. But it is another building, at Nimrud, which is more significant: in 1950 she asked for a small square, mud-brick room to be added on to the expedition quarters, for which she paid £50. The décor was hardly up to that of her houses, but it had a table, an upright chair, a comfy chair and, on the wall, two pictures by young Iraqi artists. On the door, a placard fixed in cuneiform announced that this was Beit Agatha – Agatha's House. This is where she wrote several novels and the urge to write her autobiography seized her.

One other house loomed large in Agatha's adult life, and that was Winterbrook House at Wallingford, though she thought of it as Max's house. Bought in 1935, it was a practical choice – a country cottage for weekends because Ashfield, which she had kept on after her mother's death and where they spent holidays, was too far to travel to. Except that it was not a country cottage: it was a five-bedroomed Queen Anne house, with meadows sweeping down to the river and a cedar of Lebanon in the field beyond the garden. It attracted Agatha and Max completely. Looking out on the day they viewed it in pouring rain, she was already visualizing how the lawn could be extended beyond so that the cedar tree would be in the middle of the lawn, 'and on hot days in summer we could have tea under it'. They acquired it just before a trip to Syria for a dig but did not see it again for nine months, time to become anxious about the purchase, but it proved an ideal choice, and yet again Agatha turned her hand to interior design, decorating the dining room, an important room in the house, in one of her favourite colour schemes, pale mauve with white.

A.L. Rowse's description of a visit to Winterbrook, many years later, on 'a crisp golden day' in November 1969 encapsulates – albeit with affectionate irreverence – Agatha's skill at creating a homely atmosphere. He found

a cosy, warm, hospitable middle-class interior with all the comforts and amenities, the pretty china and good furniture that Agatha's prosperity had brought. Better still, the warm, generous, kindly atmosphere both radiate. Max has (Austrian) charm and kindness; Agatha, large-chested, full-bosomed English comfortableness plus the American strain of generosity. Wine-coloured autumn sun came flooding in the blowsy, cosy room – the too-large billowing chairs (like Agatha), the lavender colour of the slagware on the chimney-piece. She brought out piece after piece of old china for me, nothing spectacular . . . just pleasant Victorian pieces (again, like Agatha herself).

On another visit, he eulogizes the cosiness and the warmth of his welcome. 'The dining room is small with rather low Victorian French tapestry chairs, good silver. There is always good food, they both like their food and have second helpings – today a favourite of Agatha's – boiled silverside and dumplings.'

But Agatha's heart always remained in Devon, the steady core of her life. By the end of the thirties, though, things had

Winterbrook House, a Queen Anne house by the river in Wallingford in Oxfordshire. Agatha always considered it to be Max's house – and it was particularly convenient when Max was made a Fellow of All Souls College, Oxford, in 1962.

changed with her home in Torquay. The house on the edge of the country had become part of the suburban sprawl. Villas around had been demolished, a mental nursing home was now next door and a school was built in front of Ashfield, blocking the view and introducing constant noise into her retreat. Ashfield, reflected Agatha, was not the place it was. Then in 1938 she found Greenway, 'the most beautiful property on the Dart – the ideal house, a dream house'. When Max suggested that she sell Ashfield in order to buy Greenway, she was shocked, but her eventual agreement was a liberation, enabling her to move on from her childhood home. Greenway became as important in her life story as Ashfield had been. As we will see later, it was a fitting destination for someone so enthusiastic about the whole process of home-making.

Even though she had made the decision to leave Ashfield, she was horrified by the news of its impending demolition in the early 1960s. Indeed, she charged her solicitor, John Wollen, with a late attempt to purchase it back. His son and successor in the family practice, Nigel Wollen, said: 'I remember my father telling me how attached Agatha was to Ashfield. I remember him going to the Council to try to persuade the Council not to demolish it in the 1950s, because Agatha wanted to buy it back. But it was a very late bid. She was very, very upset when she couldn't.'

Agatha's self-avowed passion for houses furnished her with material for her novels as well as providing her with a lifelong occupation. *Endless Night*, written when she was in her mid-seventies, is a powerful and unsettling story of obsessive fascination with 'one house in particular, a beautiful house, a house that would be wonderful to own'. Gypsy's Acre, was, says Michael Rogers, the young narrator, 'the best thing in the world. The thing that mattered most to me. Funny that a house could mean that.'

ABOVE Agatha and Max at Greenway with two of Rosalind's Shia-tzus.

RIGHT Greenway seen from the Hydrangea Walk above the house.

She talked about her views on houses in an interview with Francis Wyndham in the *Sunday Times* in 1966. One thing that infuriated her, she said, was the complaint that she always set her novels in country houses, which, as she pointed out, was not actually true. But she added: 'You *have* to be concerned with a house, which is where people *live*.'

THE HOUSEHOLDS – SERVANTS AND STAFF

'Skivvy indeed! I'm a Household Help, a Professional
Domestician, or an Answer to a Prayer, mainly the latter.'

As an upper middle-class household at the turn of the twentieth century, Ashfield had its full complement of staff. As Agatha Christie points out, servants were not an exceptional luxury in those days: 'It was not a case of only the rich having them; the only difference is that the rich had more.' Where her household might have differed from some others was in the attitude of respect that prevailed: Agatha recalls her mother reproving a young visitor for being casually discourteous to a servant. And a major component of the young Agatha's life was her relationship with servants.

The outstanding figure in her early life was her nanny. 'Dear Nursie – I have a portrait of her hanging in my home in Devon,' she wrote in her autobiography. As carer of the child of the house and ruler of the nursery, Nursie was in a different category from the other members of the household. There are still 'Nursies', or their modern equivalent, in many young children's lives, but no longer maids and cooks.

After Nursie, in order of importance to Agatha, came Jane the cook, who ruled the kitchen with 'the calm superiority of a

queen'. Having arrived as a slim girl of nineteen, newly promoted from kitchenmaid, she left forty years later, weighing 15 stone (95 kilos) – not surprisingly, judging by the account Agatha gives of the kitchen, one of her favourite parts of the house, where Jane presided over lavish teas and crisp, curranty rock cakes served hot for elevenses.

Throughout her life Agatha had a strong appreciation of servants, citing the five-course dinners for seven or eight Jane cooked most days, and the choice of courses at grander dinner parties. But it was not only the cook whose work the young Agatha noted: there was the parlourmaid who supervised matters in the dining-room, as well as the housemaids who lit fires, mended linen, took hot water to bedrooms several times as well as filling and emptying hip baths – 'we had a bathroom but my mother considered it a revolting idea to use a bath others had used'.

Her observations provide a useful insight into middle-class life at the turn of the twentieth century, but also give a revealing glimpse into Agatha's attitudes as she goes on to commend the professionalism of servants: 'Servants in the early 1900s were highly skilled . . . servants were appreciated – as *experts*.' They had, she said, prestige.

The Morning Room at Greenway, now painted in the cream that Agatha Christie herself chose when the house was first decorated in the late 1930s.

4.50 from Paddington, published in 1957, is set in a house that was inspired by Abney Hall, the home of Agatha's sister Madge and her husband James Watts.

Her acknowledgement of the status of servants percolates throughout her books, and reaches its apogee with her portrayal of Lucy Eylesbarrow in *4.50 from Paddington* (published in 1957), the Oxford-educated young woman – with a First in Mathematics – who chooses a career as a housekeeper. She had 'hit upon a very serious shortage – the shortage of any kind of skilled domestic

labour'. But her choice was not simply motivated by money, as she took pride in her work: 'Cooking satisfies my creative instincts, and there's something in me that really revels in clearing up mess.' And when disparaged by a man of the house, she replies: 'Skivvy indeed! I'm a Household Help, a Professional Domestician, or an Answer to a Prayer, mainly the latter.'

Similarly, Agatha was not above considering domestic work as an option, if need be. When she accompanied Archie on a round-the-world working trip for ten months and had to consider the possiblity of funds running out, she was certain of her ability to earn a living, if necessary, as a parlourmaid. 'A tall parlourmaid never had any difficulty in finding a job, and I was quite sure I was well enough qualified. I knew what wine glasses to put on the table. I could open and shut the front door, I could clean the silver – we always cleaned our own silver photograph frames and bric-à-brac at home – and I could wait at table reasonably well.'

Her confidence in this respect was echoed by the heroine of her third novel, *The Man in the Brown Suit*. Anne Beddingfield was undaunted by having no money at all after buying a boat ticket (first class, of course) in pursuit of adventure and announced her intention, if need be, to become a parlourmaid. There was a great demand in South Africa. Of course she did not actually have to resort to this approach – and nor did Agatha – but the willingness was there.

The presence of servants in Agatha's books is sometimes crucial to the storyline: they are used as a tactical device in that they are seen but not observed, and are therefore often crucial witnesses to events. But her descriptions also give a revealing glimpse into the changing make-up of households. The house at Styles, in 1916, had a large staff including the parlourmaid, Dorcas, who with her grey hair rising in stiff waves from under her cap was the very model of 'a good old-fashioned servant', but Styles in wartime had been left with 'only' three gardeners. In *Sleeping Murder*, written during the Second World War, the establishment of an ex-army

Bells for the servants at Greenway.

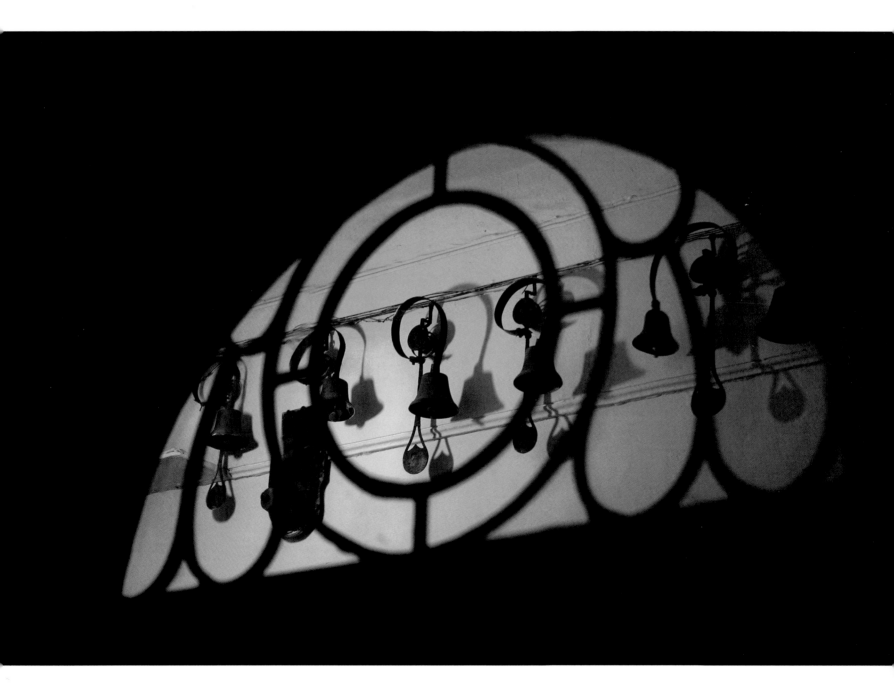

major can still sustain a decent staff: when Gwenda needs a car moving, she rings the bell and the servant fetches another who touches his cap and drives the car into the stable yard. *After the Funeral* (1953) registers the changing circumstances with the advent of daily cleaners and the old butler's disapproval of the new young cook who has 'no dignity and no appreciation of his, Lanscombe's, position'. By the time of *Nemesis*, published in 1971, the Old Manor House sustains only one elderly servant.

In *The Murder of Roger Ackroyd*, published in 1926, the outline of alibis of members of the household (excluding the butler, Parker) made by the inspector investigating the case lists – in order of precedence, no doubt – Miss Russell the housekeeper, Ursula Bourne the parlourmaid, Mrs Cooper the cook, Elsie Dale the housemaid, Gladys Jones the second housemaid and Mary Thripp, the kitchenmaid. Oh, and Mary Black, the lodge keeper. It seems a great number of staff for what does not look like a particularly grand establishment: the diagram of the house layout a few pages previously shows a ground floor comprising study, drawing room, dining room and billiard room.

The parlourmaid, Ursula Bourne, plays a significant part in this novel, almost – one could say – above her station. (Please look away now, if you have not read the book.) Indeed, it turns out that she comes from a family of impoverished Irish gentlefolk, and rather than becoming a nursery governess – 'the one profession open to an untrained girl' – she chose to be a parlourmaid: 'I enjoyed the work. And I had plenty of time to myself.'

Though Agatha retained a considerable admiration for the work of servants, she is not unvaryingly respectful. In *The Murder at the Vicarage* she does not show quite the same deference to their skills: she refers to Mary, the vicar's all-purpose servant, as 'a truculent dimwit'; has Lawrence Redding being derogatory about his cleaning woman; and describes Gladys, the kitchenmaid at the Old Hall, as more like 'a shivering rabbit'.

Agatha herself employed a variety of staff over the years. When she set up home with her first husband Archie, accommodation had to be made for his batman, Bartlett, a common enough arrangement in those days. The most famous batman-turned-servant was Lord Peter Wimsey's Bunter in Dorothy L. Sayers' books, who ensured that his master was perfectly dressed, cooked excellent meals and dealt faultlessly with social etiquette. It is not recorded whether Bartlett lived up to such high ideals, though Agatha called him 'a kind of Jeeves' and observed that his service was excellent.

For Agatha, after Rosalind's birth in 1919, there was 'my dear Devonshire Lucy', who had worked at Ashfield before joining the WRAF during the war. When she heard that Agatha was going to have a baby, she declared herself ready to move in as soon as she was wanted. After consultation with her mother, Agatha decided to offer what was for a servant 'an enormous sum in those days' – £36 a year. (For comparison, Archie's salary with a city firm was £500.) Then there were the nannies. 'Looking back,' Agatha wrote in the very different world of the 1950s, 'it seems to me extraordinary that we should have contemplated having both a nurse and a servant, but they were considered essentials of life . . . the last things we would have thought of dispensing with.'

The first nanny was Jessie who, though kind to Rosalind, was 'one of those who by nature' dislikes the parents of the child they are looking after. She was followed by Cuckoo, so called by the toddler Rosalind and then everyone else in the household, who, with her constant stream of talking, managed to stop Agatha working; and later Marcelle, who had bunions and could not take long walks with Rosalind, as well as being a hopeless disciplinarian. One way and another, Agatha paints quite a fraught picture of the difficulties of having staff. But she also inspired great loyalty. Carlo was in her early twenties when she came to work for Agatha and remained with her until her retirement.

At Ashfield, after Agatha's mother's death, Florence Potter was the cook and housekeeper for fifteen years, staying on from Mrs

The Aga in the Kitchen at Greenway.

The Dining Room at Greenway with, at the far end, one of the unusual mahogany doors curved to fit in with the shape of the room.

Miller's days. It was to Florence that, while clearing the house after her mother's death, Agatha presented the 'large wax-flower crown' under a great glass dome that had been her grandfather's memorial wreath and which Agatha felt unable to discard.

In an interview by Colleen Smith in Torquay's *Herald Express* in 1990 to mark the centenary of Agatha Christie's birth, Florence's son Freddie remembered his mother's provision of up to four meals a day on a daily basis during the summer months, and the seven-course meals she would often cook when Agatha was entertaining. One of her specialities was apple hedgehog, a pudding decorated with blanched almonds; other favourites were banana creams and coffee gateau. Freddie and his mother lived in the cottage that

had been converted from the coach house next to Ashfield, and he had free rein to wander though the house and grounds. He recalled 'eerie' memories of stuffed animals in glass cases, chintz-clad furniture, marble effigies and a grandfather clock – and also the huge gardens in which he would play and climb trees with Rosalind. At Easter, there would be an egg hunt, with a chocolate Easter egg hidden in nooks and crannies throughout the garden for everyone, including staff – and Peter the dog.

Agatha wrote in her autobiography about a mishap Freddie had with Peter. It was the weekend when Max Mallowan visited Devon for the first time (and proposed to Agatha before returning to London): 'Rosalind greeted us with her usual bouncing good spirits, and immediately announced disaster. "Peter," she said "has bitten Freddie Potter in the face." That one's precious resident cook-housekeeper has had her precious child bitten in the face by one's precious dog is the last news one wishes to hear on returning to one's household.' But all was settled amicably. One assumes that it became a cheerful memory as, when Florence eventually left to open a guesthouse, Agatha gave her a copy of *Dumb Witness*, in which a wire-haired terrier Bob, very like Peter, has a starring role and which is dedicated "To Dear Peter, most faithful of friends and dearest of companions. A dog in a thousand.'

In *Come, Tell Me How You Live,* based on the digs in Syria with Max between 1935 and 1937, Agatha wrote of running a household: 'The servant problem is very different from the servant problem in England. You might say that here the servants have an employer problem. Our fancies, prejudices, likes and dislikes are quite fantastic and follow, to the native mind, no logical pattern whatsoever.' Why the mistress of the house should be so concerned about the tea towel being used to clean mud off a radiator, or that the washing up was dried with a sheet ('But it is a dirty sheet'), was a matter of puzzlement to them, as were the intricacies of table-laying to the houseboy Mansuer: 'Even at tea, the simplest meal, his arrangement of a single fork does not meet with favour. For some inscrutable reason we demand, at a time when there is nothing serious to cut, a knife! It simply does not make sense.'

Nevertheless, despite all odds – and the environment – Agatha managed to ensure that proper English meals were provided, and inducted the cook into the mysteries of making lemon curd ('a great success') and a vanilla soufflé, though the shortbread was so inedible it had to be buried, and the Chicken Maryland was horribly tough.

The Second World War changed many aspects of households. But Agatha required staff not only for her establishments but also for the market garden she set up at Greenway after the war. After advertising in *The Times*, she wrote to an applicant, Mrs McPherson: 'I have a good Head Gardener and two under him – but need someone to drive a car and trailer to market stuff in Torquay and Paignton, also some of the hotels – To keep

accounts and all entire charge of the financial side – wages etc – and do a certain amount of practical work in greenhouses and gardens etc – since the selling only amounts to about three days a week.' The salary offered was be £5 10s. 0d. a week, as well as a commission on sales, and accommodation would be in 'a furnished cottage overlooking the Dart – two bedrooms, sitting room, kitchen and bath'.

Mrs McPherson was appointed, but within a year it became clear that this was a disastrous decision, which, in Agatha's absence with Max, was remedied through the joint efforts of Rosalind, her husband Anthony Hicks and Edmund Cork who wrote to Agatha: 'Mrs McPherson was not at all what you wanted.' In successive visits Rosalind and Anthony, Edmund and the accountant Mr Heaven managed to unpick the damage, which included bills for £800, 'lots of it for improvements to Ferry Cottage'. In the Edmund Cork archives at Exeter University there is a bundle of identical letters, each accompanying 'a cheque in settlement and Mrs Mallowan much regrets the circumstances in which this credit was obtained in her name'.

Bert Brisley, the then head gardener, had, in Edmund's view, no commercial expertise either, as his only object was 'to give you what you like: there is an exceptional crop of peaches and they are almost ecstatic as to how much you will enjoy them.' This was, as Edmund pointed out, not the point of the enterprise.

Bert had to go too, though according to John, their son, also interviewed for the *Herald Express* Agatha Christie centenary edition, his parents lived on for a while in the lodge at the gates of Greenway before they moved to their own home in Paignton, which they named Tweenaway. The replacement garden staff got things back on to an even keel, but there were often problems in retaining staff at Greenway in what became after the war primarily a summer home.

One member of staff who remained for several years was George Gowler, a butler and factotum at Greenway in the 1950s.

Glasses and Scotch – from Anthony Hicks's extensive collection of malt whiskies.

Later in his life, he made a bit of a living by giving talks about his time in service there; and in the archives housed in the long low room over what used to be the stables at Pwllywrach, the home of Agatha's grandson Mathew Prichard, is a typewritten monograph by him, headed 'In the Service of a Great Lady, The Queen of Crime'. In it, he recalls how he came to work for Agatha. He was actually a chef, but he saw an agency advert for 'a butler and his wife working for a writer'. He attended an interview at Agatha's flat in Swan Court and, over a cup of tea, was hired for the post.

Undaunted by his lack of experience, he had a stroke of luck on his way down to Greenway, when he found at the Paddington station bookstall a little booklet entitled *How to be a Butler* 'and that was the start of my new career'. He had the uniform already – a rather distinguished one, as it had been the actor Michael Wilding's tailcoat. 'All I had to buy was a pair of pin-striped trousers and a black waistcoat.'

All went well for a while, but then he said to Agatha: '"I could really do with a £1 a week rise". The response I received was not dissimilar to the reply that Oliver had when he asked for More.' So Gowler left – to work first for a countess and then for a household in Derby; but when his wife's grandfather died he had to return north with his wife to Kirkby Lonsdale to sort things out and look after her grandmother. It was a frugal time, so 'cap in hand I wrote to Agatha and told her the situation and said I would love to come back and work for her if she would have me. She welcomed me with open arms and no mention of how I had left before.'

Gowler and his entourage drove down to Devon in a van with 'Granny's bits and pieces including the budgie and the television', arriving at five in the morning. 'By 10am we were all established. We felt as if we had never been away. When Agatha came down to see us, we went about our business as if we had never parted. Granny settled in nicely and when Agatha used to come down they would have long chats together, they had a lot in common together because their age group was similar.'

His account is peppered with insights – about the television (the only one at Greenway, so on occasion the family crowded round it in his room), the wine kept in the boathouse, the continuing Easter tradition ('eggs were decorated and hidden under rhododendrons and round the lawn'), learning how to serve caviar and the fact that Agatha was a whizz at making mayonnaise ('She would always come into the kitchen and make it herself'). She was also 'a marvellous carver. We would buy a full saddle of lamb, the sort of thing you don't see today, and Agatha always insisted on doing the carving at the table.'

Life trundled on pleasantly for Gowler. 'I had free range in the kitchen to do what I wanted and also had an open chequebook. Most of our produce could be ordered in Paignton, but we went

Agatha at Winterbrook. Though she usually employed a cook, she closely supervised menus and, at Greenway, would insist on making the mayonnaise herself.

As the collection of household china was
catalogued during the restoration of Greenway,
each item was carefully cleaned, measured,
assessed and labelled.

AGATHA CHRISTIE AT HOME

to Brixham for lobsters and we used to have some lovely Dart salmon.' Agatha, he remembers, was very fond of desserts and all sweet things: 'rice pudding made with cream, apple pie and scones for tea. She had a lovely orchard garden with all kinds of fruit including dates and figs.'

The highlight of the day was the meal at night, which could last for up to two and half hours. This was preceded by drinks in the library ('there was no smoking. Agatha never drank or smoked'), and then followed a ritual of Gowler's devising. Twenty minutes before dinner he would strike the gong, dressed according to how he felt:

If I was in the mood when everything had gone right, I would put on my full Butler's uniform, and if it was a day when it was a bit messy, I would wear black trousers and white coat. But you could depend on it that every time I struck that gong one person would come out of the library where they were having drinks and see what I was wearing. If I was wearing my full Butler's uniform it meant dressing up for dinner. If I was in the white coat it was casual. This was a tradition, it was never mentioned. I don't know how it was created but I put it down to another of those mysteries surrounding Greenway House.

In his monograph, Gowler also recounts a game – an echo of that played in Agatha's grandmother's house in Ealing – he was in charge of during the dessert course: 'There were 17 plates with all different fruits on and I used to go round and put the plate down in front of each person and place a serviette on top.' Mathew Prichard remembers this well: 'Magnificent plates each decorated with a different fruit. For some years this was orchestrated by Gowler who used to hide the faces of the plates with a linen napkin and finger bowl and would rigorously allow each guest his favourite plate once a week.' Agatha's favourite was the fig, but even she was rationed.

What Gowler particularly enjoyed, however, was the part after the meal when the bell had been rung to signal the end of eating. 'Nobody would stand up until I had opened the door and then they used to troop down to the lounge graced with a magnificent grand piano. Agatha was a marvellous pianist.' His biggest thrill was to walk into the lounge with the coffee 'on a lovely Georgian tray. When I picked that up and walked into the lounge nobody knows how I felt.'

In the long winter evenings, he learnt how to do tricks and would sometimes be called on to entertain the party. 'You see, I didn't think of Agatha as my employer, she was a friend. We seemed to be a family, all knitted together.'

Eventually he left to take up a position at a hospital – as Greenway was a holiday home, he missed the company the rest of the year. The solution to the servant problem, eventually, was to employ a cook-housekeeper: A.L. Rowse commended the 'very good' one he encountered. 'She tells me that Wallingford is far better than Greenway for milk, cream, butter, poultry, provisions – in Devon the best is skimmed off to London.'

In 1965, when she was writing the final pages of her autobiography, Agatha regretted the fact that, when the alterations had been made to Greenway, she had not gone further and eliminated the huge kitchen areas, once required for the army of servants of earlier times: the enormous larder, the store for firewood, the numerous sculleries. She thought she should have instead installed a small kitchen close to the dining room. 'It never occurred to me that there would be a day when there would be no domestic help.'

In Agatha's lifetime the whole pattern of domestic service had changed utterly, in her own life and as reflected in her books. When she visited America in 1966, she told a reporter: 'When I reread those first books, I'm amazed at the number of servants drifting around. And nobody is really doing any work, they're always having tea on the lawn.'

THE HOME TOWN – TORQUAY

'A fashionable winter resort enjoying the prestige later accorded to the Riviera.'

Today all that remains to mark the spot where Ashfield stood in Torquay is a blue plaque, which Agatha's grandson Mathew Prichard unveiled in March 2007. Commissioned by the Torbay Civic Society and financed by an anonymous private donor, it reads: 'To commemorate the site of "Ashfield". Birthplace and first home of Agatha Christie (née Miller), Writer and playwright 1890–1976.' It is set in a plinth of stone standing on the pavement by the bus bay on Barton Road. There is no trace, no sense at all, of the spacious grounds that surrounded the home it commemorates. The gardens and woodland have been overlaid with dull square buildings, flat pocket-handkerchief lawns and boxy bits of hedge. There is nothing left of them to see.

But a journey here is not wasted: it was only when I walked up the slopes of Barton Road, past yet more building sites and turned back to look down the hill to the sea far below that I appreciated the wonderful vantage point of this spot and its importance for Agatha – and her distress when the school was built. Her haven

Wounded soldiers, in 1915, arriving at the Pavilion in Torquay to be entertained. It was after a concert at the Pavilion, built in 1912 as 'a Palace of Pleasure', that Archie Christie proposed to Agatha.

of tranquillity had been invaded and she could no longer even catch sight of the sea from the house that had been so important a part of her life landscape. I could understand her dismay. On a brilliant late summer day, the sea was shimmering far below, sunlight glancing off the crests of the waves, colours shifting constantly, but I could merely glimpse it between the buildings of an ever-extending town.

At the turn of the century, when Agatha was a child and Torquay was 'a fashionable winter resort enjoying the prestige later accorded to the Riviera', Barton Road led almost immediately into the countryside. By the 1930s, this was no longer the case: it had become part of the urban sprawl. Now, climbing up Barton Road to this point and past what was Ashfield, there are bungalows with steeply pitched roofs, small blocks of flats, infant roads leading into new conclaves of housing and freshly built terraces stepping up the hill: long lines of suburban housing in its pleasant innocuity.

Later that day, I walked with a fellow bus passenger from the stop on Brixham Road towards Churston church, another landmark in Agatha Christie's later life, during her Greenway days. I told him of my visit to the site of her home in Barton Road. 'Fancy that,' he

Princess Pier, next to Torquay Harbour, was a favourite spot for recreation.

said. 'I lived in Barton Cross and I never realized she had lived so close.' Then, looking back to his own youth, he said with a sense of recognition: 'It must have been wonderful for her, the sea in front and Dartmoor behind.'

It was an illuminating comment, indicating the specialness of a place that was in Torquay but almost out of it too. When she was a child, she would walk into the Devon lanes with her nurse to pick primroses. When she was older, she used to walk down the hill and round the corner to Torre station to set off for trips to Dartmoor. Torre station is still there, its neatly eaved timber railway buildings reputedly designed by Brunel, but now, disconcertingly, an oak furniture showroom. It continues as a stop for trains to Newton Abbot, but no longer to Dartmoor. The

close-meshed network of railways lines that can be seen on maps of the South Devon Railway era has disappeared, though a couple of heritage steam lines staffed by enthusiasts still fly the flag. Torre station was where, after taking the advice of her mother, Agatha caught the train to go to the Moorland Hotel near Haytor Rocks on Dartmoor, where she completed *The Mysterious Affair at Styles*.

Ashfield has gone, but there are still many spots associated with Agatha, though they have mostly been transformed somewhat. One that has not is All Saints' Church, in Bampfylde

AGATHA CHRISTIE AT HOME

Road, which, its newsletter announces, has 'strong historical links to the famous author Agatha Christie'. It is linked to her in a fundamental way, as her father gave money for it to be built. The congregation had been meeting in a temporary wooden structure nearby, but Frederick Miller thought that they could do better than this and was one of the founder members of the fine Pearson-designed church, completed in 1889. There are those who come to see the church, with its characteristic vaulted ceilings, because it was the work of John Pearson, whose best-known creation was Truro cathedral. But many more come because this is the church the young Agatha used to attend. Here is the grey and pink marble font, with its eight twisted columns, in which two-month-old Agatha was baptised. On the wall, next to a picture of the foundation stone being laid and the Lord's Prayer worked in crochet lace, is the page from the parish register noting Entry 267 on 20 November 1890, the baptism by H.W. Majendie, Vicar, of Agatha Mary Clarissa, daughter of Clarissa Margaret and Frederick Alvah, whose 'rank or profession' is given as 'Gentleman'.

When she was older, Agatha would attend services. On a visit to All Saints' Church during Agatha Christie Week, which takes place in September each year, I was greeted by Hilary White, a stalwart of the parish who gives talks on Agatha Christie, recounting details of her life. 'Agatha used to come to this church with her father, and they would sit up the front and he would say after ten minutes "Would you like to go?". "*No*," she would say, "*No*."' Hilary White relayed this so categorically that I found myself looking at her doubtfully, wondering if indeed she had witnessed this event, so authentic did it sound. When I asked her how she knew all this, she explained that her English teacher at school had been a Miss Petty, daughter of the vicar of All Saints', who had been full of stories about Agatha Christie.

In her early grown-up life, Agatha retained her connection with the church. If she was dealing with an ecclesiastical situation,

she would ring the vicarage, 'and she would speak to Miss Petty and say "Is your father busy?" Her father would say, "Tell her to come down for tea." And she would come down with her mother, who wore a long black coat and black picture hat and had a black ebony cane with a silver head. And Miss Petty told me how she could hear them coming with the tap tap of her mother's cane. Agatha was very fond of her food – she was passionate about cream. There would be an Indian brass tray and a silver teapot and a cakestand with scones or whatever.' Agatha later acknowleged her indebtedness to the vicar for the finer points of ecclesiastical custom and practice when writing *The Murder at the Vicarage*.

There are more stories in the same vein. Agatha used to shop in Lucius Street, where she got her sweets in Mr Wylie's shop: 'he made his own boiled sweets, pear drops and barley sugar and she would stand there and sniff and sniff. Then there was the bakery with all its lovely smells, and in Belgrave Road there was a dairy, and she used to look at the bowls filled with clotted cream and the yellow crust on top. Later she would have it by the cupful. She would have a cup of cream by her typewriter . . .' Hilary's talks on the locations associated with the young girl, the fees for which she donates to the church, are mostly derived, of course, from Agatha's autobiography, but presented so fluently, with barely a pause. Hilary's commentary segues into her own memories: of Mr Pook who would deliver meat in a horse and cart, ringing a bell to announce his arrival, he with his polished gaiters and bowler hat, the horse all covered with brasses; and of her father – who did actually once meet Agatha in the course of his work with Totnes Rural District Council, now South Hams, when he had to go and trace the source of a spring under the lawn at Greenway. Hilary even has an anecdote about Father John Lee, the assistant priest who, when he arrived in the parish, told Hilary that he had buried Miss Marple before he left his parish in Silbury. He was, of course, talking about the actress Joan Hickson, best known for her role as Miss Marple in television adaptations of the novels, whose home was in Wivenhoe in Essex but who was buried in the village in Devon she knew well because her daughter lived there.

The former vicarage is round the corner from Barton Road, in Newton Road; now a hotel, Heathcliff House, it is a prime example of the grandeur of vicarages in the old days. The stable where as a young girl Agatha would mount her horse – Crowdy, a strawberry roan – for rides into the countryside was next to what is now the Conservative Club, adjacent to the gargantuan new police station; the Athenaeum Rooms over Callard Restaurant in Fleet Street where she attended dancing classes are long gone; and the theatre that so entranced her and perhaps influenced her play-writing career became a cinema.

Many of the places associated with her in Torquay, however, remain intact, and are marked by plaques on the Agatha Christie Mile, a walk along the seafront visiting landmarks in her life, based on research – and sometimes guided – by Joan Nott, a redoubtable Blue Badge guide, who was one of the first to capitalize on Torquay's association with Agatha Christie and has made it her speciality. For those not lucky enough to experience her expertise at first hand, a map and leaflet is available from the tourist information centre. The route includes Beacon Cove, then a Ladies' Bathing Beach, where Agatha often swam when she was young – and almost drowned one day – and is overlooked by the Royal Torbay Yacht Club, which was a home from home for Frederick Miller. He would adjourn there every afternoon to play cards, read the newspapers or meet friends, except during the summer season when, as president of the Barton Cricket Club, he would shift his focus to the ground. It was probably at the club that Frederick Miller met the solicitor Cecil Wollen, then Commodore of the Royal Torbay Yacht Club (his grandson Nigel is now Admiral of the club), who acted for Agatha's family in the purchase of Ashfield and thereafter was a family friend: 'he was perhaps a father figure: he was the same age as her father,' said Nigel.

Palm trees and the Pavilion, with its copper-covered domes and ironwork, added to Torquay's status as a fashionable resort.

The Agatha Christie pilgrim can then walk down to the harbour, with its tightly packed boats, and across its elegant new silver pedestrian bridge to the Edwardian splendour of the copper-domed Pavilion which, now a shopping mall, was once a grand concert hall, attracting the most eminent of conductors. This was the location for a crucial date for Agatha. On 4 January 1913, she attended a Wagner concert there with the young officer she had met three months before, Archie Christie. After returning to Ashfield that evening, Archie proposed – or, rather, issued an ultimatum – to Agatha: 'You've *got* to marry me.'

Close to the Pavilion, which features in a Tommy and Tuppence story, 'Unbreakable Alibi', are the Princess Gardens (where the prime suspect in *The ABC Murders* sits on a bench) and Princess Pier, named after Princess Louise, daughter of Queen Victoria. The pier was a favourite spot for Agatha, for there she would

Agatha Christie (centre) in a feathered hat, roller-skating on Princess Pier with her friends, the Lucy family. She broke off her engagement with Reggie Lucy to marry Archie Christie.

ABOVE LEFT Torre Abbey, the oldest building in Torquay and once a monastery, is now a museum and gallery. In the grounds is a 'poison garden' in memory of Agatha Christie.

ABOVE RIGHT Torquay Museum, built in 1876 for the Torquay Natural History Society, of which Agatha's father was a member, now has a gallery devoted to her life and work.

rollerskate with her friends the Lucy sisters and their brother Reginald. Later, she would play golf with him on the cliff-top course – and received a proposal of marriage from him there – that inspired the first scene in *Why Didn't They Ask Evans?*.

Set back from the seafront is Torre Abbey, founded for the Premonstratensian Order in the twelfth century and once its wealthiest monastery. It became a home in the seventeenth century for the Cary family, who were Roman Catholics when to be so was a bad idea (there was a secret chapel in the roof). They remained there until 1930, when the abbey was sold to Torbay Council and opened to the public. There is no record of Agatha having visited the Carys at Torre Abbey, though it is likely that the

Millers and the Carys knew each other, but for several years until its renovation it had a memorial room dedicated to Agatha.

Torquay Museum is now the prime place in Torquay to find out more about Agatha; and it has another connection, as Frederick Miller belonged to the Torquay Natural History Society, for which the Grade II listed building was opened in 1876 to display many of the discoveries made by founder member William Pengelly. Now one of the galleries is devoted to Frederick Miller's daughter, with books, costumes, maps and photographs illustrating the connections between the author's life, her home town and her novels. One, for example, of Fleet Street, clearly shows a photographer's shop, Rose K. Durrant and Son, which appears little changed as Durrants in *Postern of Fate*. Also on display is the record card detailing her service at the Red Cross Hospital: Torquay Town Hall, grand and imposing at the junction of Union Street and Marychurch Road, is the site of the dispensary where she learnt about poisons, and crafted *The Mysterious Affair at Styles* – in which one of the characters, Cynthia Murdoch, also works at a Red Cross Hospital.

RIGHT Agatha's Red Cross record card from the time she worked for the hospital in the Town Hall during the First World War. It is now on view in Torquay Museum.

BELOW The Old Town Hall of Torquay with its Italianate clock tower was replaced in 1913 by a larger building at Castle Circus.

NURSING MEMBERS , COOKS, KITCHEN-MAIDS,
CLERKS , HOUSE-MAIDS . WARD-MAIDS,
LAUNDRESSES, MOTOR-DRIVERS. ETC:

ARE URGENTLY NEEDED

APPLICATION TO BE MADE TO

		PERIOD OF SERVICE, Etc.
Surname	*Christie*	
Christian Names	*Agatha* (Mrs.) (Mr, Mrs. or Miss)	From *Oct. 1914* To *Sep. 1918*
Permanent Address:	*Ashfield - Barton Rd*	
	Torquay.	
Date of Engagement	*Oct. 1914* Rank *Nurse* Pay *nil*	*Town Hall Red Cross Hosp:* *Oct: 1914 - May 1915*
Date of Termination	*Sep. 1918* Rank *Dispenser* Pay *£16 per an*	*Torquay* *June 1916 - Sep. 1918*
Particulars of Duties	*nursing first, dispensing afterwards*	
Whether whole or part time, and if latter No. of hours served	*3400 hrs.*	
Previous Engagements under Joint War Committee, if any, and where	*nil*	
Honours awarded	*nil*	

As befits a resort that attracted celebrities – Elizabeth Barrett Browning, Charles Darwin, Rudyard Kipling (who struck up a friendship with Agatha's parents during his stay in Torquay) – along with holidaymakers galore, Torquay described itself as 'the Queen of Watering Places' (just as now it has become the English Riviera) and specialized in fine hotels. The *ABC Railway Guide* of 1952 carries advertisements for twenty-five of the best, and the Torquay seafront is bookended by the two finest. The Imperial ('here is Mediterranean living without Continental currency', says *ABC* 1952), up on a promontory close to Beacon Cove, is magnificent, with its enormous chandelier in the entrance hall, and gracious curving staircase. The Imperial appears in Agatha Christie's books occasionally as itself but also as the Majestic: in *The Body in the Library*, after the shock of finding the victim in her house, Dolly Bantry declares that a few days at the Majestic is just what she and Miss Marple need. It was here, on the terrace overlooking the bay, that Miss Marple gave her final explanation in *Sleeping Murder*, the last book to feature her, and where Poirot sat in *Peril at End House*; though the town is named as St Loo

ABOVE The Imperial Hotel, on the headland overlooking Torbay, was the first five-star hotel outside London. In the background is Rock End House, location for *Peril at End House*.

LEFT The terrace of the hotel, where Hercule Poirot first met the owner of End House, and where Miss Marple unravels the mystery in the closing scene of *Sleeping Murder*.

RIGHT Entrance hall of the Imperial Hotel.

in Cornwall, it is clearly identifiable as Torquay since it is described as 'the Queen of Watering Places' and reminds Captain Hastings, Poirot's friend and amanuensis, of the Riviera. Poirot meets the owner of End House (based on Rock End House, a house along the cliff) which has a short cut to the hotel. In real life, a walk along the terrace now shows a set of steps disappearing into a rhododendron bush, and a former exit filled in with grey breezeblocks. The route to Rock End House is now impassable.

Built in 1866 by a consortium headed by Nigel Wollen's great-grandfather – his grandfather and father were in turn chairmen of the hotel – the Imperial reached the heights of being the only five-star establishment outside London. It was sold in 1970 and is now part of the Barceló chain (and has four stars). With its superb perch above Torbay, bedrooms with expansive balconies, public rooms with mirrored doors and delicate moulding on the ceilings, it retains much of its splendour (and sells nine varieties of bottled water).

The Grand Hotel is on the seafront ('No hills to walk up', *ABC* 1952), opposite a luxuriously sandy beach which, at low tide, reveals an expanse of green seaweedy rock, attracting gulls and paddlers, all searching for cockles.

LEFT The Edwardian splendour of the Grand Hotel, close to the station and overlooking the sea, where Agatha and Archie Christie spent the first night of their honeymoon.

RIGHT The Old School House at Cockington village, one of the many thatched buildings preserved as it was in the 1930s.

The Grand is the striking white-turreted Victorian building where Agatha and Archie spent the one night of their honeymoon. They had married the day before in Bristol by special licence at Emmanuel church, asking a passer-by, Reginald Fourdrey, to act as witness with Archie's stepfather (though in her autobiography Agatha says the passer-by turned out to be an acquaintance, Yvonne Bush). Frederick Miller's profession on the marriage certificate is again given as 'Gentleman' (but the second marriage certificate of 1930 has him as 'Fundholder'). Agatha and Archie then caught a train to Torquay, arriving at midnight and crossing the road from the station to the Grand. There is now, in her honour, the Agatha Christie suite, a two-bedroomed apartment with a carpet of suitably thirties-style geometric design and a Venice–Simplon Orient Express poster – as well as a knocker and letter box on its front door.

North-west of the Grand Hotel is Cockington village, so picturesque that it has the appearance of a film set. The enclave of thatched cottages, many of them pink-washed, with a forge and the Edwin Lutyens-designed Drum Inn (also thatched) looks like the sort of rural oasis that might be associated with the fiction of Agatha Christie – a location for the St Mary Mead home of Miss Marple, perhaps – and indeed it has become an 'attraction', with a craft centre and gallery in Cockington Court and teashops. The village belonged to the Mallock family, who had a tradition of public service to the town – the clock tower at the junction of the Strand and Victoria Parade was erected in 1902 as a memorial to Richard Mallock, MP for Torquay from 1886 to 1895 – and the preservation of the village was ensured by a trust the family formed in the 1930s to retain 'entire and unchanged the ancient amenities and character of the place and in developing its surroundings to do nothing which may not rather enhance than diminish its attractiveness'.

Agatha was friendly with the Mallocks, in particular Iris, who later married into the Champernownes of Dartington Hall. In the years before the First World War Agatha would visit Cockington

THE HOME TOWN

BELOW Cockington Court, now a craft centre and gallery, was the home of the Mallocks, friends of Agatha's family and enthusiastic organizers of amateur dramatics.

BELOW RIGHT Agatha dressed in her costume for Sister Anne, her role in *The Blue Beard of Unhappiness*, performed at Cockington Court.

OPPOSITE Anstey's Cove, one of the many beaches where Agatha liked to swim, with the bathing machines that were used by women until she was in her early teens.

Court to take part in their amateur theatricals. In one, *The Blue Beard of Unhappiness*, she was cast as Sister Anne, dressed in suitably exotic Eastern attire. Also performing was one Amyas Boston, whose first name Agatha pillaged for the strong-willed artist and murder victim in *Five Little Pigs*. In her autobiography, she recalls a romantic moonlight picnic with him at Anstey's Cove, where they sat holding hands and not speaking.

Not far from Anstey's Cove is Kents Cavern where Pengelly made his discoveries, an extraordinary complex of Stone Age caves,

AGATHA CHRISTIE AT HOME

with dramatic stalagtites and stalagmites formed about 2 million years ago, and one of the earliest known sites of human life. It is described in *The Man in the Brown Suit* though, as Nick Powe (the fourth-generation owner) regretfully points out, not by name: it becomes Hampsley Cavern, 'rich in Aurignacian deposits, reindeer paintings and flint implements.' Heroine Anne Beddingfield's father, together with the curator of the small museum, spent their days 'messing about underground and bringing to light portions of woolly rhinoceros and cave bear', before he conveniently died

so that she could commence her adventures.

Torquay recurs often in Agatha Christie's novels, though masquerading under other names: as Loomouth in *Three Act Tragedy*, Cullenquay in *Mrs McGinty's Dead*, Redquay in *Ordeal by Innocence* and Hollowquay in *Postern of Fate* and, most often, as St Loo, which is also in a Westmacott novel, *The Rose and Yew Tree*; in *Evil Under the Sun*, the rowdiness of the hotels in 'St Loo' comes in for special criticism from the proprietress of the Jolly Roger Hotel.

Anstey's Cove, which was the setting for romantic moonlight picnics with a fellow performer in *The Blue Beard of Unhappiness*.

at the centre of her life for nearly five decades. Even after selling Ashfield, it stayed in her heart.

Eight years after she sold it, the longing that she still felt for it is expressed in *The Hollow:* her character Midge Hardcastle yearns for Ainswick, modelled on Ashfield, in an unusually tender passage, quite unlike Agatha's normal style:

> There was a magnolia that almost covered one window and which filled the room with a golden green light in the afternoons . . . Through the other window you looked out on the lawn and a tall Wellingtonia stood up like a sentinel. And on the right was the big copper beech.
> Oh, Ainswick – Ainswick. Those lovely days at Ainswick!

Towards the end of her life, Mr Francis Doidge, Devon Club Cricket Association Secretary, sent congratulations to her after she became a dame in 1971. In her letter of response, after a vignette of her childhood, she includes a lament for her home in Torquay:

> The cricket club was certainly a central feature of my life as a child and one that will never pass from my memory. I was extremely proud of being allowed to help my father with the scoring and took it very seriously. When I am in Devon nowadays, I often drive past the cricket ground just for the sake of memories long ago. Chapel Hill where I used to go for walks with my nurse, and a field which is now houses used to have lambs, which I loved.
> The house Ashfield where I was born and which was home for 40 to 50 years was pulled down and is now only a memory. Our beautiful trees, an enormous beech tree, many ashes, a tall Wellingtonia, all gone forever – there is still one tree – the stunted remains of a Monkey Puzzle – it sticks up bravely in a back yard.

Agatha was not above poking fun at Torquay. Lucy Angkatell, the delightful but eccentric hostess of *The Hollow,* playfully speculating about the hometown of the sisters of Gerda Christow, the dreary wife of the murder victim and the prime suspect, guesses first Tunbridge Wells, then: 'Torquay, if you prefer – no, not Torquay. They would be at least 65 if they were living at Torquay.' In *Postern of Fate*, she is no longer playful: 'Hollowquay was a has-been if ever there was.' But whatever feelings she had for Torquay, it was Ashfield that was important, occupying a position

A view of Torquay across the golf
course in front of Torre Abbey
towards Dartmoor, with St Luke's
Church on the left.

THE HOME COUNTY –
FROM DARTMOOR TO THE RIVER DART

'I begin to think of Devon, of red rocks and blue sea.
It is lovely to be going home.'

Though the Torquay of her youth had changed, Agatha Christie remained faithful to Devon until the last, and always had a home there. Apart from providing a refuge, it was the cherished location for highlights in her life: it was at Ugbrooke House, for example, a grand mansion in Chudleigh halfway between Torquay and Exeter, where she met Lieutenant Archibald Christie, who was stationed at Exeter garrison. At a ball held here in October 1912 by Lord and Lady Clifford they danced together for most of the evening, and then, shortly afterwards, he rode over on a motorbike, unannounced, to visit Agatha. It was the start of an overwhelming romance.

Devon also provided inspiration for her novels and characters. She often, for example, took names of streets or villages for her characters – Dittisham, across the river from Greenway, gave its name to Lady Dittisham in *Five Little Pigs*; Luscombe Road in Paignton gave rise to Colonel Luscombe in *At Bertram's Hotel*. Barton from her own Barton Road is used for individuals in *Sparkling Cyanide* and *The Moving Finger*.

View over Greenway with Torbay in the background.

Narracott, a hamlet near Appledore in North Devon, seems to have been a particular favourite. It crops up first in *The Sittaford Mystery* as the name of a thoughtful police inspector, and in *And Then There None* as the boatman Fred Narracott; then no fewer than three walk-on parts in *Sleeping Murder* are given the same name: the late head clerk of the Dillmouth estate agent, the 'full-bosomed' receptionist of the Royal Clarence Hotel in Dillmouth and a train passenger who lived in Woodleigh Bolton where the former maid Lily Kimble was supposed to disembark.

Occasionally, she slips in an admiring general comment through a character. 'Devon is so beautiful, those hills and the red cliffs,' said Vera Claythorne in *And Then There Were None*. Practically all the hills in Devon, according to Agatha, were just the right shape.

Ashfield, on the edge of Torquay, was the perfect starting point for forays into and across Devon. During the years – almost thirty – Agatha lived there and for the next two decades when it was her base, a fixed point in her otherwise hectic chopping and changing of abodes, she would explore the Devon countryside close to her home either on foot or on her horse, and would catch the train from Torre for Dartmoor, alone or with friends. At the other end of her life, when she was living at Greenway, she would get up

a party and drive to the beach, maybe Blackpool Sands south of Dartmouth, for swimming or up to Dartmoor for a picnic. Mathew Prichard remembers many such occasions:

> There was lots of bathing – my grandmother loved swimming. We bathed in the river at high tide, by the boathouse at Greenway or we'd go to Broadsands, where we used to watch the little local trains going over the viaduct – the Torbay Express used to go over that viaduct! – or Elberry, though that had no sand. Other times, we would go out for a picnic on Dartmoor, with a wicker hamper, in a lovely old car, a Humber Super Snipe, one of the first cars to have bucket seats and a wind-up partition.

Picnic thinking was a factor in her choice of car. She wrote to Edmund Cork: '*Room* is the thing, because of being able to get seven or eight people down to the beach or for picnics in the summer . . . pure fun is less important to me than comfort and *space*. You've no idea the amount of things archaeologists take

PREVIOUS PAGES Blackpool Sands, south of Dartmouth, was a favourite destination from Greenway for family picnics.

LEFT The Paignton and Dartmouth steam train crossing Brunel's viaduct close to Broadsands beach.

ABOVE This inlet on Burgh Island was the setting for Pixy Cove, the site of the murder on Smugglers' Island, in *Evil Under the Sun* (which curiously also features two Pixy Caves, here and on Dartmoor).

RIGHT Family picnic on Dartmoor. With Agatha are, from left, Rosalind, Mathew and a family friend, Oliver Gurney.

about with them.' Later she added: 'The car has been *heavenly*. We went eleven in it the other day to a picnic.'

Fond though she was of Dartmoor for convivial family picnics, Agatha knew its wildness and remoteness, and used that aspect to great effect, most notably, in *The Sittaford Mystery*, in which the moor is a pervasive and occasionally sinister presence. This is only partly due to the escaped prisoner, and the atmospheric bell that tolls to announce the breakout: the intention, the reader discovers later, was that Pixie's Cave at Sheepstor was to be his hideout. This cave also makes an appearance in *Evil Under the Sun* when Poirot rounds up hotel guests and takes them off for a picnic on

Dartmoor, near Pixy's [sic] Cave; it is, of course, not altruism that motivates him but the need to test a character's head for heights.

Even modern-day Dartmoor, with its very distinctive landscape, has not lost that sense of isolation: it is so close to main towns and resorts and yet so self-contained. Its mixture of high-hedged, narrow lanes interspersed with long vistas – cars on roads threading through the undulating terrain visible from miles away, the green uplands all patchworked with fields or scored with rusty bracken – lend a strangeness, an other-worldly air. With its great expanses of valleys and tors, colours ever changing, and clouds moving fast and low on the horizon, Dartmoor is continually fascinating.

Somehow, driving between the villages on the moor, even on a bright autumn day, takes on the perspective of an adventure.

That feeling is enhanced on the road leading down to Princetown, with the stern sign instructing drivers not to stop. The reason for that sits hugely in the valley below, Dartmoor prison, once regarded as the harshest in the country but now, according to the landlord of the Devonshire Arms in Sticklepath (a place Agatha must have known, as she adapts the name to Sticklehaven for a village in *Evil Under the Sun*), a mere and disappointing Category 3. It would have been a Category 1 when featured in *The Sittaford Mystery*.

There are the signs, too, of the tin mines that used to be in production here, which give a sense of the Dartmoor Agatha might have known; and another impression of those times can be gleaned from the Finch Foundry in Sticklepath, now owned by the National Trust but, with its three great water wheels, working into the 1960s. Not far away is Chagford, once a stannary town where miners brought their tin for weighing and valuing; the eight-sided Market House was the stannary court. Tucked on the edge of the moor, remoteness at its doorstep, this little town with (appropriately) its two ironmongers, a tiny bookshop (part café) and delicatessen and health food shops provides welcome respite from the great outdoors.

Along a one-track lane, seemingly miles from anywhere, lies Widecombe-in-the-Moor, with two pubs and the sixteenth-century Church House, which the National Trust has returned to its original function as village hall and focus of the community. The tower of its huge church (known as the Cathedral of the Moor), which was built by tin miners, is visible for miles around. It is not as lively as it was once, though, when it was the setting for one of Eden Philpotts' most popular novels, *Widecombe Fair* (published in 1913), a copy of which is on the bookshelves in Agatha Christie's bedroom at Greenway, along with other titles by her mentor.

The place on Dartmoor that is most associated with Agatha Christie is the Moorland Hotel near Haytor Rocks. This is the place to which she adjourned in the grip of writer's block to complete her first detective novel. She would have taken the train to Bovey Tracy and then a coach to the hotel. When she stayed there, it was fairly new, and intimately connected with the local industry of the mining of granite – granite from Dartmoor was used in Nelson's column and the original London Bridge. Lucy Lee of the Dolphin Hotel in Haytor Vale had married John Hellier, who owned a profitable interest in the Haytor Quarry, and after his death Lucy decided to use some of the wealth to build another house in 1892,

which in 1905 became a hotel with twenty bedrooms, a billiard room and lavish gardens. It was in 1916, at least in Agatha's view, 'a large dreary hotel. There were few people staying there. I don't think I spoke to any of them – it would have taken my mind away from what I was doing.'

When she wasn't working, she was walking. 'I learned to love the moor in those days . . . the Tors and the heather and all the wild part. Everybody who went there, not many in war time, would cluster round Hay Tor itself but I left Hay Tor severely alone and struck out on my own across country.'

Agatha may never have paid a return visit, but Moorlands, as it now is, proudly proclaims its links with her in the lounge, with a portrait and posters of her books on the walls, a tastefully arranged set of novels in black and the Agatha Christie Bar. Owned by HF Holidays (originally Holiday Fellowship) and run mainly for groups, it is a rather striking hotel. The lounge, for example, has walls covered in black silk taffeta and a chandelier made of Dartington crystal, originally destined for Cunard's *QE2* but brought here from the Grand Hotel in Torquay.

After Lucy Hellier died in 1932, her daughters ran the hotel until the Second World War, when it was requisitioned by the army and then bought by Trust Houses. It was a glamorous venue for some years, until a fire in 1970 laid waste to it and it was abandoned. In 1979 it was seen by a flamboyant character called Sidney Hindle, a cross-dressing millionaire entrepreneur with a chain of remnant shops in the south-west, to whom the idea of a hotel where he could conduct his risqué social life in privacy appealed. So he and his mother bought the ruin for £16,000 and turned it into a lively and idiosyncratic venue: he threw out guests he disapproved of while wearing high heels, stockings, a long black dress, pearl earrings and a long black wig. It is his taste in décor that is responsible for the lounge walls and the abundance of mirrors. Now it is a comfortable base for all sorts of respectable activities from bridge to country dancing.

Moorlands, now owned by HF Holidays but
formerly known as the Moorland Hotel, where
in 1916 Agatha finished her first detective novel,
The Mysterious Affair at Styles.

AGATHA CHRISTIE AT HOME

LEFT Thatched cottages in Haytor Vale.

BELOW Haytor Rocks, a granite tor close to Moorlands. The site of granite quarrying in the nineteenth century, it had become a great tourist attraction by the time of Agatha's stay at the Moorland Hotel.

Close to the hotel and facing the granite bulk of Haytor Rocks on the horizon is the newest of Dartmoor National Park's information centres, built of local timber and insulated with sheep's wool, and opened in 2008. The great window inside has underneath an inscription from Eden Philpotts' description of the former quarry: 'A cicatrix of moss and fern and many grasses conceal the scars of pick and gunpowder, time has weathered the harsh edges of the riven stone, the depths of the quarry are covered by pools of clear water . . . it is a testament to the capacity of nature to take over from man.'

After the First World War, when Agatha's main focus switched away from Devon and she lived in London and then in Sunningdale, she still returned to Ashfield for long periods and made excursions to other parts of Devon which later featured in her books. Burgh Island, for example, was the setting for two of them – *And Then There Were None* and *Evil Under the Sun* – and was where the 2002 television film of the latter was shot, the first

in the series starring David Suchet as Poirot to be partly filmed in the actual place Agatha Christie was writing about.

Burgh (pronounced 'Burr') Island off the coast of South Devon is linked to Bigbury-on-Sea by a wide expanse of sand, which for twelve hours a day is shallowly covered by sea. The means of getting to the island then is by a very tall contraption with high wheels and containing twenty seats under an awning – the only sea tractor in the world.

The island is only 20 acres (8 hectares), rising up to a hill where the remains of the Huer's Hut stand. From here a watchman used to spy the shoals of pilchards coming the island's way and alert the fishermen (some say the origin of the phrase 'hue and cry'). Now the point of this island is its hotel. The island, together with its fourteenth-century Pilchard Inn, was bought in 1927

ABOVE The fourteenth-century Pilchard Inn on Burgh Island stands close to the rather newer Burgh Island Hotel.

RIGHT Burgh Island is sometimes referred to as 'a part-time island', as when the tide recedes there is a sand bar linking the mainland at Bigbury-on-Sea to the inn and hotel.

by the millionaire Archibald Nettlefold, who made his fortune out of screws (over the doorway in the hotel breakfast room is an intriguing collage of a Union Jack made entirely of different styles and colours of screws in honour of Nettlefold's origins) and then went on to become a theatre impresario – which is probably how he knew Agatha Christie. He commissioned the distinctive white mansion, which is built in brilliant Art Deco style, with curlicued mirrors, geometrically designed carpets and a wonderful

LEFT AND BELOW The dining room of the Burgh Island Hotel and the corridor leading to the Ballroom with the Art Deco details that give the hotel its distinctive character.

Palm Court with a glass dome in peacock colours. For some time Nettlefold used it to entertain guests of a particularly illustrious calibre, including Noël Coward, Lord Mountbatten and the Duke of Windsor, but perhaps exasperated by their readiness to take his hospitality, he turned it into a hotel in about 1933. Soon afterwards, he added a new wing with twelve bedrooms and a ballroom, so it was obviously a successful move.

Agatha stayed there on a number of occasions, and used its location, which is near to civilization and yet utterly remote, as inspiration for one of her most ingenious books, *And Then There Were None*. The modernism of the house of the story echoes that of the hotel, and the cliffs where one victim meets his death reflect those on the island. Bigbury-on-Sea, 'a mere cluster of cottages with a fishing boat or two drawn up on the beach', becomes Sticklehaven.

But *Evil Under the Sun* is the one that is more recognizably taken from life. A walk round the island shows the accuracy of the map at the front of the book, in which the positions of the hotel, the coves and the causeway to the mainland all echo the real thing. The Jacob's Ladder in Pixy Cove that provided an escape route for the murderer actually existed. Its steel posts still remain, but the rest was removed during the war to prevent secret landings by Germans.

A 1940s advertisement relays a conversation between two men about a third – a portly moustachioed man smoking a cigarette with an air of self-satisfaction. The caption reads: ' "Cholmondely looks pleased with life!" "Of course, he's just booked his holiday at Burgh Island."' But after Nettlefold died in 1944 the hotel deteriorated, and was eventually turned into self-catering apartments.

In the late 1980s, Tony Porter (once a consultant for that iconic fashion store of the sixties, Biba) and his wife Beatrice, known as B, bought the hotel and in a nail-biting tussle with banks finally managed to finance it by selling off three houses on the island. He entertainingly recounts the battle to restore the dilapidated carcass of the hotel to its original grandeur – from B's making all the curtains in the hotel to the mending of the wrecked Peacock Dome roof by a craftsman from the Midlands – in his book *The Great White Palace*. The Porters made use of the Agatha Christie connection, naming cocktails after her books. In 1986 Agatha's daughter, Rosalind Hicks, brought a group of family and friends to partake of a cream tea on the lawn outside the sun lounge. Tony recollects her pleasure in the island and hotel but also her objection to the claim in the brochure that *Evil Under the Sun* was written on the island. Rosalind said quite firmly, 'Mother didn't write the book here. You shouldn't say she did.' The brochure was changed.

The hotel remains as beautifully individual and Art Deco as ever, with its Lloyd Loom blue-green wicker chairs under the Peacock Dome and the sloping windows of the Captain's Cabin, salvaged by Nettlefold from HMS *Ganges* and stuck on the end of the lounge. Outside is the Mermaid Pool, a delicious deep green tidal pool with a bathing platform in the middle. Down below the terrace is the Beach House, said to be where Agatha stayed. The associations with Agatha Christie have been downplayed somewhat since Tony and B Porter sold the hotel in 2002 to Deborah Clarke and Tony Orchard, who had earlier held their wedding on the island, but there is still a Christie suite.

Just down the road from Bigbury-on-Sea is the Kingsbridge estuary. For a map of this area, one can look at the first page of Agatha Christie's *Towards Zero*: the arrow towards St Loo, in the direction of Torquay, is the clincher, but its network of creeks

Below the Burgh Island Hotel is the tidal Mermaid Pool, which, with its diving platform in the centre, is a favourite spot for bathing.

LEFT The coastline around Bigbury Bay, much of it owned by the National Trust, is secluded and wild.

BELOW Kingsbridge Estuary, lying inland from Salcombe, is recognizable on the map in *Towards Zero*, in which Kingsbridge becomes Saltington.

and inlets is also clearly recognizable: Kingsbridge has become Saltington; Salcombe appears as Saltcreek, a straggling picturesque fishing village set on the side of the hill; Gull Point, the striking house at the heart of the story, stands 'white and serene' above the river, rather as Greenway does; and just as there is a ferry that plies its trade between Saltcreek and Easterhead in the book, so is there one between Salcombe and East Portlemouth.

The road round the coast down into Salcombe discloses a charming view: a bustle of boats, even on an October day, with yachts tacking across the bay, small ferries chugging back and forth. It is so *busy*. The Marine Hotel, where Agatha stayed during the war,

is the prime spot to observe all this marine activity. Interestingly, Salcombe was the location for the London Weekend Television adaptation of her *Peril at End House*, though in the book the action takes place at Torquay (or St Loo, as it is called in the book).

One place known to Agatha Christie and which, by rights but not in fact, should have provided inspiration is Dartington Hall, a magnificent Tudor mansion on the doorstep of Totnes: its Great Hall, medieval courtyard, clock tower, fourteenth-century White Bear pub (with, now, real ale, from the Otter Brewery) would have provided a perfect setting. There is, though, a sort of family connection through the Champernownes, who owned Dartington from 1559 to 1921: apart from the fact that Agatha had a friend who had married into the family, it was a Champernowne who was the first mistress at Greenway in the sixteenth century.

AGATHA CHRISTIE AT HOME

OPPOSITE The busy sailing resort of Salcombe, which appears as Saltcreek in *Towards Zero*.

ABOVE: Dartington Hall. Agatha visited it when it was owned by Leonard and Dorothy Elmhirst, and Leonard showed her round the gardens.

The last Champernowne to live at Dartington Hall was Arthur Champernowne, who moved out because of the crippling effects on the estate of the First World War and the agricultural depression, and then sold it to Leonard and Dorothy Elmhirst, who founded Dartington School along with developing Dartington's fine reputation for arts and culture. The relationship between the Elmhirsts and Agatha Christie was not close, but in the archive at

High Cross House, the striking modernist house that was built in 1932 for the headmaster of the school, is a letter from Agatha to Dorothy, expressing her gratitude to Leonard for showing her and a friend, Sir George Taylor, around the gardens and inviting her to luncheon. Whether the luncheon took place or not is unrecorded.

Much later, in March 1972, Leonard Elmhirst wrote asking Agatha to open 'a new and rather special variety of nursery school'. In her reply, in which she declines on the grounds of having given up all public engagements – 'the only exception to this has been when I did go and open the new addition to Galmpton School' (the local primary, of which she was a governor) – she remembers the friend who had married into Champernownes: 'Iris Mallock

of Cockington Court was one of my best friends as a girl, and I think Iris Champernowne was then in residence at Dartington.'

Bordering the Dartington estate and flowing past Greenway down to the sea is the River Dart. The Dart has long been famous, having been granted the royal seal of approval by Queen Victoria. In her journal, she described her visit to Dartmouth on 20 August 1846: 'Notwithstanding the rain, the place is lovely, with its wooden rocks, and church and castle at the entrance. It puts me so much in mind of the beautiful Rhine and its castle and the Lorelei.'

In fact, Queen Victoria had earlier visited Dartmouth en route from Plymouth to Torquay when she was fourteen. She is said to have avoided the seasickness of the sea voyage by using the Higher

AGATHA CHRISTIE AT HOME

Ferry, which is still in operation today under the management of the Dartmouth–Kingswear Floating Bridge Company, and was still guided by cables and powered by paddle wheels, until the replacement larger ferry came into service in 2009. But it was on her subsequent visit, when – according to local historian John Risdon, author of a

LEFT Dittisham Lake, the widest part of the River Dart and much used for sailing. On the opposite bank is the thatched Ferry Cottage, by Greenway Quay.

BELOW Paddle steamers plied their trade along the Dart, taking tourists from Totnes to Dartmouth and back again. Inspector Bland in *Dead Man's Folly* took a trip on a pleasure steamer to test out a theory of his about the murder.

book on the river – she is said to have travelled up to Totnes on one of the pleasure steamers, that the river seems to have won her heart.

There are other royal connections. Edward III, in the expansive way that royalty had in those days, bequeathed 'the Waters of the Dart' to his son, the Black Prince, who became the Duke of Cornwall in 1338. This bequest included the right to charge dues on anything that was moored or floated – a right that continues these days: Prince Charles, Duke of Cornwall, still owns all the mooring rights on the river. But the National Trust is now a big landowner, providing protection to over 11,000 acres (44 hectares) of the Dart estuary.

The river was once a thriving trade route, with salt cod, spices and camellia plants coming in, and mining products and wool

from Dartmoor going out. Once hugely busy with industry, the Dart remains full of river traffic, with a constant flow of ferries – including the diminutive Dartmouth to Dittisham ferry boats, distinctive in scarlet – and sightseeing cruises. Pleasure steamers have for years plied their trade down the river from Totnes and back again, pointing out the spot where the D-Day fleet assembled in the Second World War, the summer home of the broadcasters the Dimblebys, and Greenway. This river activity is reflected in *Dead Man's Folly*, when a cousin of Lady Stubbs of Nasse House moors his yacht in the estuary at Helmmouth (Dartmouth) and then boards a launch to visit her, and – after the inevitable murder – the investigating police officer Inspector Bland takes a trip upriver from Brixwell (Brixham) on the *Devon Belle* to test out a theory.

Once one of England's principal ports, Dartmouth is now a calmer place. At the mouth of the Dart are two reminders of its strategic past: Kingswear Castle (now available for rent through the Landmark Trust) and on the opposite bank Dartmouth Castle. The chain that used to be stretched across between them at night to deter marauders was called Old Jawbones – so says Salty, the improbably named skipper of *Riviera Belle* on the Agatha Christie Cruise, which runs from Torquay up to Greenway.

Dominated by the sandstone bulk of the Royal Naval College and with its harbour crowded with sailing ships, Dartmouth has the air of a Mediterranean seaport, its colourful houses cascading down the hillside to the river: navy blue, egg-yolk yellow and turquoise on the houses near the waterfront, and gentler pastel colours higher up. On the quay is the Royal Castle Hotel, originally built as two merchants' houses in 1639. The advertisement for the hotel on the back of an 1895 guide to the river by Robert Cranford proudly proclaims that it is, 'Patronised by Royalty.' As a postscript it adds 'Fitted with Electric Light and Bells . . . and the Sanitary Arrangements are perfect.' Agatha Christie and her family knew the hotel well – and it appears as the Royal George Hotel in 'The Regatta Mystery' and in *Ordeal by Innocence* – where Dartmouth has become Drymouth.

Dartmouth has the unique distinction of being the only town in the country to have a railway station with no railway. This came about because of a former owner of Greenway, Richard Harvey, who did many good things for the area, such as building houses for his workers in Galmpton. But what he is famous for is preventing the Dartmouth and Torbay Railway Company from taking the track through his land to cross the river at Dittisham. After taking his objections to the House of Lords, he forced the company to take trains through a tunnel under Greenway and alongside the river to Kingswear – whence passengers can take the ferry across to

Dartmouth. The people of Dartmouth were deeply antagonized by his action but the tranquillity of this corner of Devon, so much valued by Agatha Christie, is due to his intransigence.

Though enjoying the peace and privacy of Greenway, Agatha did participate in the different facets of the life of the county, taking part in local fruit and vegetable shows, delightedly receiving an award as Doctor of Letters at Exeter University in 1961 and in 1966 instituting the Mousetrap Challenge Cup at the Devon and Exeter Steeplechase and Hunter Races. But above all Devon was her home. In *Come, Tell Me How You Live* she describes how, after months on a dig, she looked forward to her return: 'I begin to think of Devon, of red rocks and blue sea. It is lovely to be going home.'

AGATHA CHRISTIE AT HOME

OPPOSITE The Royal Castle Hotel on the quay at Dartmouth appears as the Royal George in 'The Regatta Mystery' and in *Ordeal by Innocence* – where Dartmouth is known as Drymouth.

BELOW Dartmouth's characteristically colourful houses line Bayard's Cove, the original wharf at Dartmouth and where the Pilgrim Fathers rested in 1620 on their way to America.

THE PARISH –
GALMPTON AND CHURSTON

*'I am both proud and humble that I have been permitted
to offer it with the proceeds of my work.'*

Historically, the owner of Greenway held considerable sway over the village of Galmpton and had certain rights and duties. By the time Agatha bought Greenway, the estate had shrunk considerably, but she took her position as mistress of Greenway seriously, involving herself in the village and the parish. She was a regular attender at the St Mary the Virgin church in nearby Churston, and she was a governor of Galmpton Primary School, a position in which she was succeeded after her death by her daughter Rosalind. Agatha would invite children from the school for 'raspberry teas' on her lawns, and introduced an annual essay-writing competition for the Mallowan Literary Prize each year, for which she would set the subject and judge the entries. (In 2009, the National Trust announced the reintroduction of the competition.) In 1958, she opened an extension to the school and in 1971, a second one – this was the public engagement she mentioned to Leonard Elmhirst when turning down his request for her to open the nursery school at Dartington.

Galmpton and its neighbour Churston, which appears in *Dead Man's Folly* as Nassecombe, form an ancient parish bound by water to the west and the east, between the River Dart and the sea. Both villages are mentioned in the Domesday Book: Galmpton as Galmetona, from the old English term for 'a peasant who rented a smallholding', and Churston as Ceretone, 'the farm by the church'. When in 1303 the Ferrers became lords of the manor, they added their name: Churston Ferrers is still occasionally used.

To the north is Galmpton Creek, where for over four centuries shipbuilding flourished, and where Brixham fishing smacks were built, some of which can still be seen at Brixham Harbour in the Heritage Fleet of restored sailing trawlers, with names like Pilgrim, Vigilance and Provident. Brixham, still a busy fishing port, lies to the south and is where Agatha Christie and then her daughter Rosalind would go to the fish market – but is perhaps more famous as the landing place of William of Orange in 1688.

Churston station, which opened in 1861 as Brixham Road, features in two of Agatha Christie's novels – under its own name in *The ABC Murders*, when Poirot and Hastings, travelled down by the midnight train from Paddington after the murder of local landowner Sir Carmichael Clarke, and as Nassecombe station in

Brixham Harbour is the home of pleasure craft as well as the modern fishing fleet – and the Heritage Fleet of old Brixham sailing trawlers, many of which were made in the boatyards of Galmpton Creek.

ABOVE Suitcases on the platform in Churston station, where Hercule Poirot alighted in *The ABC Murders* and *Dead Man's Folly*.

OPPOSITE The Paignton and Dartmouth steam train pulling into Churston station, one of the four stations on the 7-mile (11-kilometre) line.

Dead Man's Folly, where Poirot was met by a chauffeur driving a large Humber saloon, just like Agatha's own car. Before it closed just over a century later, it was often used by Agatha and her family to arrive at Greenway. On the occasions Agatha's grandson Mathew travelled by train when he was young, he remembers the incongruity of the Torbay Express stopping at this station, 'which was no bigger than a grasshopper'.

Today Churston station is open again, at least in summer months, thanks to the Dart Valley Railway, which took it over in 1972. On the station wall, however, a map of the South Western region (with dotted lines emerging from Southampton and Plymouth labelled America, India, Egypt, Australia) shows what has been lost, such as the railway line from Torre into the heart of Dartmoor with now-forgotten stops at Teigngrace Halt, Brimley Halt and Heathfield.

When I visited Churston station as it opened up on a summer morning, trolleys of suitcases were being wheeled out on to the platform: 'Makes it look a bit more like it did in Agatha Christie's

time,' said a man in a grey suit, acting that day as booking clerk. Inside the booking hall were old trunks, a crate labelled 'valuable live dog' and racks of old railway tickets – Torre 1/8d. Paignton 2/-. The platforms under the white wooden canopies were bright with baskets of begonias, geraniums and cyclamen. Cheerful posters advertised Paignton as 'the family resort at picturesque Torbay', with stripy deckchairs and beach huts, and the advice of Great Western Railway to send luggage in advance: 'Collected, conveyed and delivered 2/- per package'.

When the Paignton and Dartmouth Steam Railway train pulled in with its eleven carriages (all with girls' names: Zoe, Heidi, Natasha, Jessica), the guard checked the passengers in, waved his green flag with a flourish and stepped on to the train (and then stuck his head out of the window to have a conversation on his mobile phone).

The station lies at a point equidistant between Churston and Galmpton. Just along the road from the station is Warborough Common, a meadow tended by a farmer, with a creeper-greened sail-less windmill. Galmpton today is a comfortably large village, with a school, pub, butcher and award-winning post office and shop. Many of its features are due to a former owner of Greenway, Richard Harvey, the wealthy copper magnate who spent much money in the mid-nineteenth century on improving the area. He added a model farm with a steam engine – the tall chimney can be seen, an incongruous intrusion into the landscape – and modernized Galmpton. (After his death, his widow Susannah provided the school.) Hunterswood, a large building stretching alongside the road down to the ferry, was built by Harvey as a laundry for Greenway.

Just past the Chapel of the Good Shepherd is Vale House, with a plaque announcing that poet and novelist Robert Graves lived here from 1940 to 1946. His sister Rosaleen was a GP who practised not far away, and while visiting her he drove through Galmpton and saw that the eighteenth-century farmhouse was for sale and, more or less on a whim, bought it and moved in with Beryl, who was to become his wife, and mother of their three children. Agatha made friends with him, introducing herself as Mrs Mallowan. She was, he thought, 'pleasant but stately', though on closer acquaintance he described her more fondly as 'a sweet woman'. On 18 June 1943, after the publication of *The Moving Finger*, he wrote a letter to her in which he surmised that the house in which much of the action takes place was inspired by Vale House – he recognized the portrayal of the cupboard under the stairs with its fishing rods and golf clubs.

Maypool, the cluster of buildings on a road forking left from the Greenway Road, is the site of the River Dart Youth Hostel (sadly only available at present for group bookings), and the model in *Dead Man's Folly* for the hostel from which visitors are for ever trying to find a short cut to the ferry though the grounds of Nasse House. (A visit to Greenway shows why they would have wanted to do so, as it is a much more direct route than by the road.) The hostel is in what was Maypool House, built for Francis Simpson, owner of a shipyard by the river in Dartmouth. It is an attractive, dusky-red sandstone gabled mansion, perched above the freshwater pool in the valley below which gave the house its name, and has a clear view down the Dart to the sea – Simpson

apparently installed a powerful telescope so that he could keep an eye on his workers.

The old carriage drive (now a footpath) leading to Greenway was by Maypool, and had the advantage of striking views down to Dartmouth and its thicket of masts, which must have impressed visitors. But in the nineteenth century a grander entrance was conducted by a former owner, James Elton, on the opposite side of the estate. At the gateway is the lodge, embellished in 1850 by the next owner, Colonel Edward Carlyon of Cornwall, who added the family emblem of the Cornish chough. The drive now comes out on to the road down to Greenway Quay on the River Dart, which marks one boundary of the parish.

Greenway Quay is a busy little transport hub – there has been a crossing point over the Dart here for hundreds of years. It is also one of the most picturesque spots on the river, with the thatched Ferry Cottage tucked in under trees behind the quay and a view, across the water, of Dittisham (pronounced Dit'sum by locals). Dittisham, which appears as Gitcham in *Dead Man's Folly* and Gitsham in *Ordeal by Innocence*, was renowned for its orchards: baskets of plums and damsons for sale would be placed outside the cottages in the autumn. Now it is better known for its famous residents, and for the flash cars pulled up on the foreshore (such as a plum-coloured Range Rover with the number-plate D1 TSM). The tone of modern-day Dittisham is rather indicated by the Anchorstone Café with its boards offering cream teas or 'cracked crabs, caught in Brixham and cooked at Anchorstone' and headlined with 'Fizz at £35. Be decadent, have with cod and chips.'

The *Greenway Bell* ferry plies its trade, when summoned, every day of the year except Christmas Day, taking passengers across the 250 yards (230 metres) of river, before it spreads out into the great curved expanse of Dittisham Lake. John Risdon speculates that this was the training ground of young Walter Raleigh and Humphrey Gilbert – favourites of Elizabeth I and half-brothers brought up at Greenway before they set out on

RIGHT Dittisham – Gitcham in *Dead Man's Folly* – seen from the top of the hill, with the Red Lion Hotel on the right.

BELOW The village of Dittisham seen from across the River Dart.

Broadsands, the nearest beach to Greenway, and a popular destination for swimming and beach picnics.

their seafaring expeditions – just as it is for young sailors today.

On each side of the river is a large bell: one outside the welcoming Ferry Inn, which features, though not by name, as the favourite pub of Merdell the ferryman in *Dead Mans' Folly*, and the other on Greenway Quay, close to a little hut selling snacks and a kennel labelled 'Dax' for the shaggy Samoyed belonging to Will Ross, one of three brothers who run the company Greenway Ferries, which has a small fleet of boats operating ferry services and trips out of Torquay and Dartmouth. The ferry also stars in the opening pages of *Ordeal by Innocence*, in which Arthur Calgary crosses the river in search of the house Sunny Point (in real life Viper's Point).

On the other side of the parish, opposite Warborough Common, is Babbacombe Road leading down to Broadsands beach under Hookhills Viaduct, which at frequent intervals in summer is picturesquely surmounted by the steam train, smoke unfurling and the air filled with the wistful wail of the train whistle. Designed by Brunel, the nine-arch viaduct was built after his death in 1859 and opened to the railway in 1864. The beach at Broadsands, its ranks of beach huts curving colourfully round the bay – scarlet, Provençal blue, turquoise, navy, sun-bright yellow – was a favourite beach of Agatha's.

A footpath leads past an old farmhouse, painted in creamy yellow and blue, with pots of flowers and a hay loft spilling its contents copiously. At Elberry Cove is the derelict bathing house erected by a former lord of the manor. Nearby, the body of Sir Carmichael Clarke of Churston Ferrers, the third victim in *The ABC Murders*, was found in a field 'overlooking the sea and a beach of glistening stones'. Notwithstanding that, Captain Hastings saw the beauty of the spot. 'All around dark green trees

AGATHA CHRISTIE AT HOME

ran down to the sea. It was an enchanting spot – white, deep green and sapphire blue.' This might sound fanciful, but on a brilliant summer's day the improbably deep blues and turquoises of the sea are heightened by the contrast with the silvery pebbles.

A little further, across the golf course, is the twelfth-century manor house, once the home of the Ferrers family and later of Lord and Lady Churston who often entertained Agatha to lunch. Next door to what is now the Churston Court Inn is the fourteenth-century church of St Mary the Virgin, which was once the private chapel for the manor. There is a welcoming notice outside the church on Wednesdays in August: 'Please come in and look round. See our boxed pews, and the East Window, a gift from Dame Agatha Christie.'

This was the church Agatha attended whenever she was staying at Greenway, and then by her daughter Rosalind until her death in 2004. During a service, the churchwardens take up positions at the front of the church at communion time, and move back unlatching the doors to the pews one by one to unpen the prospective communicants.

The thing that brings visitors here, as with All Saints' Church in Torquay, is the Agatha Christie connection. The most famous item in the church is the stained-glass Good Shepherd window over the altar. Agatha decided that she wanted to replace the plain glass of the east window, which 'always gaped at me like a gap in teeth. I looked at it every Sunday and used to think how lovely it would look in pale colours.' She planned to pay for it by allocating the serial rights for a 'long-short' story to the diocese; she would find the artist and commission the design, although as she freely admitted she knew nothing about stained glass. She visited studios, got different sketches and finally fixed on James Paterson, who had shown her his work in a church in Appledore. He had fulfilled commissions in other churches – in Brentnor and at St Peter's in Plymouth – and also in the Castle Inn in Lydford, for which he made a door featuring the three hares motif that

The Church of St Mary the Virgin at Churston, where Agatha attended Sunday services. Alongside is Churston Court, now a hotel, where she would sometimes lunch with Lord and Lady Churston afterwards.

is common in the south-west of England. He drew up a design that she admired very much, 'particularly his colours which were not the ordinary red and blue but predominantly mauve and pale green, my favourite ones'.

Agatha broke with tradition by specifying that the central figure should be the Good Shepherd, which was resisted by both the Diocese of Exeter and Paterson, who insisted that the central pattern of an east window had to be the Crucifixion. However, she won her case, saying, 'I wanted this to be a happy window which children could look at with pleasure.' The final version has Jesus and his lambs in the centre, with side panels of fishermen, the Virgin with the Child and the nativity starring – as Bob Bowling, an ex-churchwarden, points out – a purple cow looking over the shoulder of St Joseph.

Many years later, Sylvia Stevenson from the congregation at Churston church met James's widow, Margaret, who told her how, when Agatha commissioned the window from her husband, they were very poor – so poor that his workshop was the attic, where he made the window in sections. It was only when he went to the church at Churston with the finished parts that he discovered the identity of the woman who had commissioned him, for she had made the commission as Mrs Mallowan.

Agatha asked that there be no indication that she was the donor, though later a plaque was unveiled by her daughter saying that Agatha Christie Mallowan DBE gave the East Window 'to the glory of God'. But there is no clue in the church as to which story yielded the money. Altogether, there has long been a bit of a mystery about that, and about the circumstances of the gift. The booklet 'Churston Story', on sale in the church, says: 'Before the installation of the window … the Church authorities had to "sell back" the story to her literary agents for £1000, thus losing the permanent copyright of a work by the world-acclaimed playwright and author, Dame Agatha Christie.' The belief persists with members of the congregation that the rights to the story were snatched back after the realization that the gift had been too generous: what had seemed an act of munificence had been thought better of later. In fact, the truth was quite different.

Things had started trickily in 1954. Edmund Cork wrote to the secretary of the Diocesan Board of Finance at Exeter, putting forward Agatha's suggestion and referring to a precedent. He explained that there had been a 'similar arrangement with the Chapter of Westminster by which certain rights in an Agatha Christie story were vested in the Dean and Chapter for the benefit of the Save the Abbey Fund, and by doing it this way, the Fund benefited by the total proceeds of the exploitations of the rights without deduction of Income Tax which of course in the case of a successful writer as Mrs Mallowan makes all the difference.' At that stage Edmund cautiously intimated that the exact amount could not be specified, but he was optimistic that there would be enough to pay for the window and any balance could go to 'some suitable fund for church restoration in the Diocese'.

The pompous reply that came from Michelmores, the Diocesan solicitors, rather set the tone for the negotiation thereafter, asking a series of questions and ending: 'We must look to Mrs Mallowan through your good selves for payment of our proper legal charges in this matter, and we shall be glad if you will kindly confirm that this is understood.' Edmund Cork not unreasonably suggested that the fees should be paid out of the proceeds of the sale of copyright.

The story in question was 'Greenshaw's Folly' (a confusingly similar name to that of the quite different – and unpublished – story 'The Greenshore Folly', of which more will be heard in the next chapter), which can be found in *The Adventure of the Christmas Pudding*, a collection of short stories finally published in England in 1960. What had given Agatha the idea for the donation was a story that she had written for the Westminster Abbey appeal fund. That story had been 'Sanctuary', which appears in *Miss Marple's Final Cases*, a truly appropriate story set, as it is, in a church and with the stained-glass windows playing a powerful bit part. 'Greenshaw's Folly' does not have that synchronicity of subject, though it also stars Miss Marple. It is, however, rather longer than usual for her stories. And therein lay the problem. For, as it turned out, she was unable to sell the serial rights. Its length meant that it had to be a two-parter, and it was submitted as such by her American agent, Dorothy Olding of Harold Ober Associates, to *This Week*, the publication to which she frequently contributed. However, on 3 October 1955, its editor, Stewart Beach, wrote to Dorothy Olding expressing his dissatisfaction with it in its present form. He then enclosed two pages of suggestions as to how the Queen of Crime, then at the peak of her powers, should alter the story. For a start, he said, Miss Marple should be brought in at a much earlier stage . . .

Agatha was having none of it, and Edmund Cork wrote back to Harold Ober Associates, urging them to try elsewhere: 'This hold-up is the very devil as the Bishop and his Diocesan Council are continually on at me wanting the cash. So I do hope you'll be able to sell the story to someone else or if not tell me frankly and we will see if we cannot set up the window some other how.'

Cork spent an increasingly desperate time trying to find some way out of the impasse. The window had been commissioned and was being made, and he was being regularly harried for payment by the solicitors of the Diocese of Exeter. Confronted with the unviability of this particular 'long-short', on 6 February 1956 he wrote to Rosalind Hicks, a trustee of Agatha Christie Ltd (the company that had been set up to ameliorate her tax position), setting out the problem: 'We have run into a snag as our American people have not been able to sell it to any of the magazines over there. This means that the magazine rights in the story are unlikely to produce as much money as is required for the window and Agatha has gone some way over it in approving designs.'

He suggested that 'a way of getting out of this difficulty' was 'by Agatha Christie Limited buying the Bishop's rights for One Thousand Pounds. This would be enough to pay for the window and to pay the costs of the Bishop's solicitors who are fussing about same in a most unspiritual fashion.'

The trustees agreed to this solution and in a letter to Rosalind of 31 May he confirmed that the solicitors, Michelmores, 'have obtained the Seal of the Diocesan Board of Finance to the endorsement of the Assignment by which Agatha Christie Ltd takes over the magazine rights of GREENSHAW'S FOLLY from the Ecclesiastical authority. All we need to do now is send them a cheque.'

Cork's solution was ingenious and effective, but one which – as can be seen – was capable of misinterpretation. None of this frantic activity behind the scenes is evident in Agatha's serene account of the new stained glass in her autobiography, finished a decade later. 'I love it and enjoy looking at it on Sundays. Mr Paterson has made a fine window. It will, I think, stand the test of the centuries because it is simple. I am both proud and humble that I have been permitted to offer it with the proceeds of my work.'

The stained-glass window that Agatha Christie commissioned. Jesus Christ as the Good Shepherd is in the centre with, from left, the shepherds, the nativity, fishermen mending their nets and Jesus walking on the water.

THE HOUSE –
GREENWAY AND ITS GARDENS

*'It is the loveliest place in the world – it quite
takes my breath away'*

For years, passengers on the River Link cruise ships from Totnes to Dartmouth have gazed up at Greenway, pointed out to them by skippers as the former home of Agatha Christie, and speculated on its indefinable allure. It is in a striking position, on a promontory surrounded on three sides by the jade-green waters of the River Dart. A gracious creamy-coloured Georgian mansion, and partially screened by its mature trees and wild woodland gardens which tumble down to the river's edge, it is, though very visible, a remote and private place.

In 2000, Agatha's daughter Rosalind Hicks, her husband Anthony and her son Mathew jointly agreed to give Greenway to the National Trust. 'It was not easy to make the decision,' Mathew has said. 'We did so for one reason above all – stability. Greenway is a staggeringly beautiful place, and the Trust was the most likely catalyst to preserve and enhance that beauty for the benefit of the wider public.' The gardens opened to the public in 2002, and in 2005, after the deaths of Rosalind and Anthony, the National Trust embarked on the £5.4 million restoration,

'Another Chapter', appointing a local building firm, Coopers of Plymouth. In the spring of 2009, it opened to the public.

Greenway had been in Agatha's family since 1938, when Agatha noticed that a house she knew about was for sale: she described it in her autobiography as 'a house that my mother had always said, and I had thought also, was the most perfect of the various properties on the Dart.'

She thought it would be fun to go and have a look, as she had called there with her mother when she was a child – presumably to visit Thomas Bolitho MP, who lived there from 1882 to 1919 – so she already had an idea of its charms. She may also have felt the pull of the garden, which must have recalled the woodland garden at Ashfield. There were added attractions too: the boathouse – on the spot where, it is said, Walter Raleigh, smoking tobacco, had water thrown over him by a servant who thought he was on fire – and the battery, with its low parapets and two small cannons pointing out to the river. Sixty years before, it had been a huge estate: when it was offered for sale in 1882, it had comprised 757 acres (300 hectares), including the Manor Inn, several 'capital farms with excellent farmhouses and homesteads', as well as a long river frontage and the right of ferry across the Dart. It had been

View up the River Dart from the gardens of Greenway.

parcelled off since and pretty much all that remained by the time Agatha saw it was the 'well-appointed family mansion, beautiful well-arranged pleasure grounds, large walled gardens containing capital glass houses and hanging woods'. But 'beautifully situate on a lofty eminence above the famous River Dart', it was still a very desirable property.

Greenway was as lovely as Agatha had remembered and Max thought the setting 'idyllic'. In his memoirs, he dubbed it a 'little paradise', describing the 'foreground of steep, grassy banks and a backcloth of dark conifers. The mild climate has made it a haven for magnolias and rhododendrons; great oak trees mask the house from the river, not far from it is a walled camellia garden with one cork oak, *Quercus suber*, and the drive is flanked by beech trees 150 years old on one side, eucryphias, magnolias, rhododendrons and azaleas on the other.'

Agatha asked the price, and was astonished by the answer, thinking she had misheard £16,000 as £6,000. But it really was only £6,000. She and Max drove away discussing the house and the price excitedly: 'It doesn't look in bad condition either; wants decorating, that's all.'

That, of course, would not present a major problem for Agatha, with her experience and enthusiasm. But first she asked Guilford Bell, a young architect and a member of a family she had made friends with many years before in Australia, to look over it. His advice was to pull half of it down, as the back addition was Victorian. The billiard room, the study, the estate room – all could go. It would, he said, be a far better house, far lighter.

So, with that advice, on 28 October 1938, the conveyance for Greenway – with garden, stables, paddock and pasture – was signed by A.M.C. Mallowan in the presence of her solicitor C.J.H. Wollen. Agatha was, as usual, very involved with the alterations, taking particular interest in the bathrooms. She accompanied Guilford on one expedition, saying: 'I want a big bath and I need a ledge because I like to eat apples.'

ABOVE Greenway after its restoration.

OPPOSITE The Hydrangea Walk leads from the Fernery between box hedges towards the Top Garden.

The Mallowans did not have long to enjoy Greenway before war broke out. In 1940, while Max was working for the Anglo-Turkish Relief Committee in London, Agatha spent most of her time at Greenway, working hard – she produced two books and several stories, undeterred by the encroachment of war. She wrote to Edmund Cork: 'A great deal of air activity here – Bombs all round are whistling down! I think they were going for a Hospital Ship . . . near us in the Dart. We saw a fight right overhead the other day – and our pilot came down by parachute.'

For a while Max returned to Devon, where he joined the

Home Guard at Brixham and became increasingly interested in horticulture, ordering copiously from the Robert Veitch nursery in Exeter. He kept a planting book from 1941 to 1971 to note the trees, flowers and shrubs he had added to the garden, often with great abandon: one consignment alone included rhododendrons, Judas trees and lilacs, as well as several varieties of camellia and magnolia, of which he was particularly fond. But 'finest of all' was a *Magnolia campbellii* he planted by the tennis court, 'which if February is mild yields a thousand crimson blooms'. It flourishes to this day.

Agatha kept up a steady stream of letters to Edmund, reporting on the progress of her work, demanding stationery supplies and sympathizing with the difficulties of wartime. 'Life must be absolute Hell for you in London . . . Try and survive! We've had a few delayed action bombs near us but definitely we are out of the conflict zone though we had a good invasion scare last week . . . the house is now full of soldiers practising what they would do *if* the Germans landed – they can hardly move they've got so much on. Max has been out for nights watching for rubber boats.'

For a while in 1941 Greenway served as a home for ten children evacuated from St Pancras under the care of a Mrs Arbuthnot. At this point, Agatha returned to London and began work for University College Hospital in the dispensary. Max had, to his delight, been taken on by the Air Ministry and was sent in 1942 to Cairo.

Then came unwelcome news. On 31 August 1942, Agatha wrote to Max: 'Now to real life and unpleasant everyday facts. The Admiralty are taking over Greenway. It's been mooted for some time but is now definite. I hope they will let me keep two rooms . . . to store furniture in. I do hope they won't be destructive to trees, shrubs etc.'

The following year, the house was finally requisitioned for use as officers' quarters for the United States Navy; the sailors stayed at Maypool House. On 9 March 1943, Agatha was wondering whether to go down to Greenway that weekend. '*So* lovely in

spring there that I think it will just upset me. As it is, I've put Greenway out of my mind until the end of the war when you and I will go back together. Magnolias! Camellias! The River. And foxy old Hannaford swinging the lead as usual!'

In fact, the gardener, Hannaford, did his best for her in his own way when she finally relinquished Greenway that October, impounding huge quantities of apples and onions for Agatha, though she had no idea how to make use of them. While there, she used up her last colour film so that there would be a record 'in case anything happens', but she had been reassured somewhat by Commander Kirkwood's concern for the unusual curved mahogany doors.

'I stayed for a little while after the men had gone and then I walked up and sat on the seat overlooking the house and river . . .

The Library at Greenway with
the frieze painted by Lieutenant
Marshall Lee when he was
stationed here with the United
States Navy during the war, when
the house was requisitioned by the
Admiralty.

AGATHA CHRISTIE AT HOME

it looked very white and lovely – serene and aloof as always. I felt a kind of pang over its beauty. I thought tonight sitting there – it is the loveliest place in the world – it quite takes my breath away.'

The occupation by the Americans left no lasting damage – apart from the fourteen lavatories, to remove which she had to do battle with the Admiralty in 1945. And she was pleased with one addition – a frieze in the library, painted in subtle dark blues and beiges. The Admiralty offered to paint it over, but Agatha refused, replying that it would be a historic memorial – and, indeed, one that was particularly apt for an establishment that had such maritime connections. Depicting all the places where the flotilla went, starting at Key West, moving on through Sicily and Salerno, it ended with 'a slightly glorified exaggeration' of the woods of Greenway and the house just visible through the trees. 'Beyond that again is an exquisite nymph, not quite finished – a pin-up girl in the nude – which I have always supposed to represent the hopes of houris at journey's end when the war was at last over.'

Moving back in and setting the house straight was time-consuming and frustrating. In an old exercise book she scrawled lists of things to pack and items to buy, such as dusters and carpet for her bedroom. On a visit in spring 1945, she wrote to Max: 'Chaos at present and lots of problems. But oh! I did wish you could been there for it was the perfect time for the white magnolia below the house – and the stellata – the camellias out and primroses everywhere.'

When she and Max finally returned together, the garden was completely wild. 'How beautiful Greenway looked in its tangled splendour; but I did wonder if we would ever clear any of the paths again, or even find where they were.'

Though Greenway became principally a summer holiday home, one thing Agatha was serious about was the market garden that she set up after the war. There were teething problems. Edmund Cork's one and only visit to Greenway (he followed his late employer Hughes Massie's advice about not getting too

One of the many woodland paths in the gardens.

close to his clients) was in Agatha's absence to sort out the disaster following the appointment of an unsuitable administrator. He found time to praise Greenway in his letter to Agatha. 'I have never seen anything so lovely as Greenway was; the freshness and the graciousness of everything was a dream; but it is a big expensive dream which increasing costs have made extremely difficult to carry on. If major expenses can be paid out of untaxed income then it is alright, but the tax people are unconvinced that the present basis is a reasonable commercial one, and confidentially I am of the same opinion.'

In late May, he wrote to Agatha again to say that he had had a letter from the accountant, Mr Heaven, saying 'that it is most necessary to get the Gardens organised on a commercial footing as the Inspector of Taxes persists in asking awkward questions, obviously with the intention of showing the Gardens are nothing more than a hobby'.

By the end of the year things were on a more even keel. A new administrator had been appointed and in December Agatha wrote to Edmund: 'Just came to Greenway. The Garden looks wonderful – all bursting with plants, lettuces. It really does look professional at last.' The market garden flourished, and Agatha took great pride in its achievements, entering the local flower and produce shows with gusto, and winning lots of prizes. In his book *The Mousetrap Man*, director (of *The Mousetrap*, obviously) Peter Saunders singled out her involvement with the Brixham Show for his tribute to Agatha, 'this quiet, friendly, shy, gentle lady who has sold more books than Shakespeare. Her modesty is typified by the time she won nearly all the prizes at a local fruit and vegetable show. Asked the secret of her success, she replied "My gardener".'

Frank Lavin was her head gardener then: a story in one of the scrapbooks now on display in Greenway tells how he would engage in a game of bluff at the shows, only bringing on the real competition entries at the last minute. One year Greenway carried off so many prizes that Agatha instituted the Agatha Christie Cup for future years, a competition which her gardeners could not enter, in order to give other people a chance.

While engaged to some extent in community affairs, Agatha relished the seclusion of her home. This was on the whole respected by villagers – who knew her as Mrs M – though she occasionally let off steam about intrusions, from autograph-hunters or, one occasion, a party of Finnish journalists. And she could be kindly, as when John Risdon's young sister was caught poaching holly from the estate by Agatha: after her reprimand, she was invited in for tea.

The history of the house continually fascinated Agatha: one note she made on the meaning of the name Greenway reads: 'Named because of the "grain way" across the Dart. Belonged to Gilbert family. Sir Humphrey Gilbert. discoverer of Newfoundland. Born there c 1537. His mother's second husband was a Raleigh . . .'

The mother of half-brothers Humphrey Gilbert and Walter Raleigh, Katherine Champernowne, was mistress of Greenway Court, the medieval predecessor situated to the rear of the current building and a wall of which remains, and Humphrey's brothers, Adrian and John, contributed to ensuring that this estate in this corner of Devon had a profound input into Tudor history. They were key movers in the defeat of the Spanish Armada, providing three ships from Dartmouth. The capture of the Spanish galleon *Nuestra Senora del Rosario* was a pivotal moment. Towed first into Torbay and then to Dartmouth, it became the responsibility of Sir John Gilbert, a deputy lieutenant of Devon. The sailors were imprisoned in the old barn at Torre Abbey (to this day known as the Spanish Barn) before being moved to Greenway, where they were put to work levelling ground and/or building walls, depending on which version you believe. (Certainly the mellow walls in the camellia garden look old enough to date back to the time of the Armada.)

It was the connection with the Gilberts and the Raleighs that enticed the historian A.L. Rowse to Greenway. Agatha invited Commander Walter Raleigh Gilbert of Compton Castle over to Greenway with his wife to meet him; and on another occasion she took Rowse to see the flamboyant, turreted and battlemented medieval fantasy on the outskirts of Torquay, lived in by Gilberts from the fourteenth century until 1785 and then bought back by the commander in 1931 and rehabilitated. On his visit to Greenway, Rowse noted that Gilbert had 'sniffed round' the foundations and wall of Greenway Court. 'Agatha said "let him have his way about Greenway and he'll rebuild it too."'

Rowse was captivated by the 'rose-red' Compton Castle and the 'romantic story' of Gilbert's saving of Compton Castle. He wrote in *Memories and Glimpses*, 'As a young Dartmouth cadet he used occasionally to have a farm-tea with the farmer who owned the Castle, then more than half a ruin. Gilbert determined that one day he would restore the home of his ancestors – and lived to do it.'

Leslie Rowse, as Agatha was now on close enough terms to call him, was also attracted by her patriotism for Devon and the West Country, adding with easy familiarity that she had 'bought Mary Bolitho's Greenway' (as a Cornish family, the Bolithos were known to Rowse, an ardent patriot himself). He gave his seal of approval: 'a fine Georgian house, Greenway was in a splendid situation on a bend of the river Dart, with a view right down it, steamers passing and a magnificent garden full of the rare shrubs the West Country can grow.'

He received many urgings by Agatha to visit from his summer home in Cornwall. One read: 'This is written on Devonshire paper though we are still at Wallingford, but we go down tomorrow. I shall be there until October so do ring us up if you *can* come over anytime. I know it's quite an undertaking from St Austell – we went there to lunch once and were an hour and a half late.' On another occasion she invited him to stay for a wedding anniversary celebration. He was impressed by Max's gift to Agatha – 'his classic work on Nimrud with its astonishing illustrations, specially bound in two large morocco and gold volumes' – but what he noted most was the 'good fare Agatha provided wherever she was (she was a good trencherman: a fine Devon turkey and Devonshire cream)'.

From the early days of Agatha's residence, Greenway was known for its hospitality and house parties. Mathew recalls 'spirited arguments' between Agatha and Peter Saunders on the plausibility of certain plots. 'I remember Allen Lane of Penguin Books who arrived in a Bentley Coupé, and Billy Collins with great big bushy eyebrows, arriving almost apologetically with a typescript under his arm which, like most publishers, he wanted back the day after tomorrow.' It was, he says, the English country house at its best.

Peter Saunders was a regular visitor. In his autobiography, he recounted his first visit during the run of *The Hollow* in 1951:

Family dinner in the small dining room at Greenway. Opposite Agatha is Max Mallowan; on her right is her daughter Rosalind; on her left is her grandson Mathew and his first wife Angela; and just visible behind Max is Anthony, Rosalind's husband.

There is a delightful informality about staying at Greenway House. The gong goes for breakfast but guests go down whenever they want and help themselves from heated trays on the sideboard. After breakfast, Agatha said, 'We do exactly what we like in this house. Most of us play cricket in the morning.' It seemed a very odd pastime for this rather middle-aged gathering but it was for the benefit of her eight-year-old grandson Mathew Prichard. The house had a cricket net and we all took turns in bowling at Mathew, excepting Agatha, who declared herself umpire. Every time he was out, Agatha called 'No Ball'.

Peter Saunders observed on his subsequent visits that Mathew got better and better: 'I liked to think we sowed the seeds of his success as a cricketer.' Mathew went on to be captain of the Eton

Eleven and came within a few runs of scoring the first century for fifteen years in the 1962 match against Harrow.

In later visits, croquet replaced cricket. 'Agatha was a great enthusiast and her voice could be heard booming across the lawn. I am a bit shaky about croquet terms but it sounded something like "you ran a good hoop" and "that was a jolly good peel".'

Mathew remembers travelling with his mother and stepfather from Wales across country to Devon for the long summer holidays in 'an almost wooden Hillman Traveller – the ones with wooden slats', with the dogs in the back, to see 'Nima', the name that had stuck after he had so dubbed his grandmother in his childhood. One of his first ever memories was of Greenway and 'rushing downstairs far too early in the morning with my two soft cuddly elephants, Butterfly and Flutterby, and being told fantasies about their life in the jungle by Nima in bed'.

Although Greenway had become very much a holiday home, at times Agatha did work there. In 1950, shortly after her sister Madge had died at the end of August, Agatha wrote to Edmund Cork requesting him to send some typewriting paper to Greenway: 'You see I mean to work.' But she was discreet. Her son-in-law, Anthony Hicks, once wrote: 'You never see her writing. I would come to Greenway for a visit and she was the perfect hostess, always there, always joining in. She never, in the whole time I knew her, suddenly got up and said "I must go and write now" and shut herself away like other writers do.'

Later, there was no actual writing – she would have written the annual book in Beit Agatha or elsewhere and would, at most, be correcting proofs – but there would be readings of her latest book to members of the household. Max once put his foot in it by guessing the murderer in *And Then There Were None* – though, as he said in his memoirs, for quite the wrong reason. That put Agatha out somewhat.

In *Agatha Christie: Official Centenary Celebration,* published in 1990, Mathew wrote evocatively of these reading parties, recalling the year when she read a chapter or two of *A Pocketful of Rye* (1953) after dinner:

All the family sitting round the drawing room at Greenway, coffee cups empty, a little cigar smoke rising from my grandfather's cigar, mauve chintzy covers on the chairs and a piano in the corner of the room, Nima sat in a deep chair with a light directly above her, and her spectacles, a strange butterfly shape, were pushed slightly forward. After every session except the first two or three, we were all invited to guess the identity of the murderer . . . my grandfather Max usually finished his cigar and went to sleep during the reading, waking up with a start when we were guessing. He then consistently and obstinately plumped for the most unlikely suspect and went to sleep again.

The solicitor Nigel Wollen too has fond memories of being entertained at Greenway:

My father became a great friend of Agatha's. We were entertained often at Greenway, invited down for lunch and dinner parties – some formal, some less so. Agatha would play the piano. The last time I saw her, I'll never forget it. Sir William Collins the publisher was there. I was told to go and sit next to her in the drawing room. It was soon after Lord Lucan's disappearance, and she said to me 'Do you think Lord Lucan did it?' You could see the plot developing in her mind. I never saw her again. That was six or nine months before she died.

Greenway had been made over in 1959 to her daughter Rosalind, who moved to live in the house with her husband Anthony Hicks in 1968. After Agatha's death, Rosalind carried on looking after her mother's work, always protecting her reputation and, on rare occasions, opening the house to Agatha Christie fans. Then in 2000 she and her family made the decision to involve the National Trust. There was much work to be done in those early years by the Trust on winning round the opinion of the locals, who were afraid of a constant stream of traffic along the narrow high-hedged lanes. Project director and property manager Robyn Brown announced the decision that visitors arriving by car could only do so by pre-booking, and drew up plans for 'green ways' to arrive at Greenway, in particular by using the Dart: 'It's been a jostling river for centuries, transporting people up and down the river – so we want to use what is already there. And we encourage this by giving a discount to visitors arriving this way.' (In 2008, 40 per cent of the visitors came by boat.) Then there was all the work on preparing the gardens, a mixture of unusual plants and

The *Riviera Belle,* which runs from Torquay to Greenway, is one of the many ferries that bring visitors to Greenway.

Agatha Christie At Home

LEFT The garden at Greenway has long been renowned for its exotic – and colourful – half-hardy shrubs and trees from all parts of the world,

BELOW The vinery in the walled garden has been painstakingly restored and is now in full use again.

rare shrubs underplanted with native wild flowers, for opening to the public eighteen months later.

Greenway's gardens were already well known because of its nursery, which had evolved from the market garden. It was particularly famous for its camellias – over a hundred varieties were on sale there. (In 2007, camellias from Greenway were transported en masse to the wedding of Mathew and his second wife Lucy.) The success of the nursery was in large measure due to Anthony Hicks, who was an enthusiastic collector of such varied plants as passionflowers, orchids and the Chilean bellflower (*Lapageria rosea*), the national flower of Chile. In this, he was following in the illustrious footsteps of earlier owners such as Thomas Bolitho and his daughter and son-in-law, Mary and Charles Williams, who had planted many exotic plants. Many remarkable trees flourish here, such as Chilean myrtle (*Luma apiculata*), a Chinese fringe tree (*Chionanthus retusus*), a tulip tree (*Liriodendron tulipifera*) and black bamboo (*Phyllostachys nigra*). Near the old arch by the camellia garden is one of the oldest trees, a cork oak (*Quercus suber*) that is reckoned to be 300–350 years old.

Now there are three gardeners – including Jeff Andrews, who has been working there for approaching fifty years and comes to work each day by ferry from Dittisham – who work to keep the gardens 'on the edge of wildness', as Nick Haworth, head gardener, says. On Friday afternoons, one or other of the gardeners leads tours, through the restored vinery, past the old glass peach houses fronted by fig trees, up to the top lawn, once used for clock golf and edged by a border of dahlias planted by Agatha, and down to the river. There, in an arbour with a semicircular seat, Agatha liked to sit and enjoy the view. There is a story the gardeners tell, heard from Frank Lavin, that she decided she would like to have something more to look at and asked him to plant daffodil bulbs. Of course, when they came up they faced away from her, towards the south and the sun – and so she asked for them to be taken out again.

The gardens are full of surprises. In a sheltered position by a pond is the bronze statue of Kwan Yin, Buddhist goddess of mercy, the work of Nicholas Dimbleby. In a meadow overlooking the house, is *Mother and Child* by another local sculptor Bridget McCrum – her home on the opposite bank of the Dart is visible from here. *The Greenway Bird*, also by Bridget McCrumm, stands long-legged by a pool planted all round with *Gunnera*, which is, and looks like, giant rhubarb. Even the garden benches, sited at strategic points round the gardens, are individual: the iron legs are formed of the initials A and C, and the arms of G.

ABOVE LEFT A bronze statue of Kwan Yin, Buddhist goddess of mercy, a sculpture by Nicholas Dimbleby, stands by a pond near the boathouse.

ABOVE RIGHT In the Camellia Garden is one of the garden's distinctive benches: the arms are formed by a G for Greenway and the legs by AC for Agatha Christie.

OPPOSITE The battery with cannon overlooking the Dart, a setting Agatha Christie used in *Five Little Pigs* and *Dead Man's Folly*.

In a shady upland glade is the fernery, a dim, secluded garden of rocks of limestone and quartz, with a short flight of steps leading nowhere, many paths and a Coalbrookdale memorial fountain, made of dark-green cast iron, two tiered with a pleated edge, which Susannah Harvey installed as a memorial to her husband. It also serves as a pet cemetery: a cluster of small gravestones up on the top of the rockery commemorate Rosalind's Shia-tzu dogs: Bangle, aged eighteen, Shan Mei, 1986, Tashi 1975–88.

Down by the river is the battery – a peaceful vantage point despite the cannons – from which one can see the Anchor Stone, a rock on which scolding wives were said to have been tied. Readers of Agatha Christie's novels will recognize the battery as the place in *Five Little Pigs* where Amyas Crale met his end, and where Poirot meets Mrs Oliver in *Dead Man's Folly*; and the nearby boathouse as the setting for the murder of Marlene Tucker, the hapless Girl Guide, in that book. There is no longer a thatched roof, but the little wharf (now with a faded wooden sign: 'All persons landing on this quay or trespassing in the woods will be prosecuted') and storage place for boats underneath – as well as the basket chairs in the room above – are just as described in *Dead Man's Folly*, published in 1956.

BELOW The room in the boathouse, with wicker furniture chosen by
Agatha, and its balcony and arched windows overlooking the River Dart.

OPPOSITE The boathouse, scene of a murder in *Dead Man's Folly*, seen
from the River Dart.

AGATHA CHRISTIE AT HOME

There has been a boathouse here for centuries, but the present building is nineteenth-century. By 1839 the boathouse had been recorded as a place where guests could 'take the tidal salt waters of the Dart'. The bathing does not look very appealing, with steps leading down to the plunge pool from a dim cellar, though with a couple of pretty curved windows and matching *trompe d'oeil* windows. But upstairs is a light and airy room with a fireplace, wicker furniture installed by Agatha and a balcony over the river. Mathew remembers sitting on that balcony with his grandmother 'to watch the steamships from Torquay and Brixham go up to Dittisham. It's funny the things that stick in your mind: it's fifty years ago now but I still remember the names – *Western Lady, Brixham Belle, Pride of Paignton. Kiloran* would come last and then we would go back to the house for Devonshire cream tea. She used to drink cream from a huge cup with "Don't be greedy" written on the side, an injunction she never showed any sign of obeying.'

Greenway had made an appearance in Agatha's fiction before, as Alderbury in *Five Little Pigs*, but *Dead Man's Folly* could act as guidebook for the estate. The surroundings of Nasse House (which even Poirot approves of) described in this book mirror exactly those of Greenway, from the beautiful river view with 'hills of a misty blue in the distance', which Poirot is invited to admire, to the position of the neighbouring youth hostel.

Dead Man's Folly was expanded from an unpublished story, 'The Greenshore Folly'. The 108-page typed manuscript has been corrected in Agatha's handwriting, mostly to make the names of the places less identifiable. Devonshire remains but Churchtown – perhaps too close to Churston – has been changed to Laptown. In *Dead Man's Folly* it becomes Nassecombe, and Greenshore House, Nasse House. The River Dart of the story becomes the Helm in the novel and the youth hostel changes from Upper Greenshore to Hoodown Park – though there is still a clue to real-life location as the name comes from Hoodown Woods just a short distance south, near Kingswear.

The descriptions of the house and gardens are recognizably of Greenway. The lodge in the novel, where the former owner of Nasse House Mrs Folliat lives, is a small white one-storeyed

ABOVE View from Greenway over the River Dart.

OPPOSITE The Drawing Room at Greenway with Agatha's writing desk, where she wrote her letters, against the wall near the window.

building, set a little back from the road, with a small railed garden round it – just as in real life (it has recently been restored by the National Trust from the state of dilapidation into which it had fallen). The layout of Nasse House, with a small sitting room on the left of the front door leading to a big drawing room, is that of Greenway. The paths meandering down to the quay – with its bell for the ferry – and through the woodland gardens, utterly confusing for Poirot ('So many paths, and one is never sure where they lead. And trees, trees, trees'), are all identifiable.

At one stage it seemed that the gift to the National Trust would entail simply the gardens and the house, without its contents. But Robyn Brown talked to Rosalind about the desirability of having some of the possessions in the house to convey the atmosphere of Agatha's time as well as Rosalind's and Anthony's, so that visitors could, as Robyn put it, "'see your mother at play; we'd like to show it as if you and Anthony had just stepped out into the garden". I told her, "It just wouldn't be the same without the sense of the life you all lived here."' She had to assuage Rosalind's fears that the house would become an 'Agatha Christie experience': 'I needed to reassure her that there wouldn't be Poirot in the library or Miss Marple in the sitting room.'

Her gentle persistence won the day, and Rosalind's agreement was obtained. After her death, Mathew offered the most important items to the Trust – 5,000 of them, along with nearly 5,000 books. And, with the help of a grant from the Heritage Lottery Fund, the major task of conservation of the collections began. Everything had to be removed, cleaned, measured, assessed and labelled by staff and volunteers. In the process, discoveries were made – such as the identity of the pair of old chairs from the inner hall, painstakingly cleaned with orange sticks and warm soapy water. Tessa Tattersall, one of those cleaning the chairs, had guessed that they were made around 1600 and then had a 'eureka' moment when reading in Janet Morgan's biography of how Miss Marple got her name, from Marple Hall in Cheshire. 'It said that Agatha and Madge had gone to a very good sale of fine Elizabethan and Jacobean furniture at Marple Hall, and Agatha bought two fine Jaobean dark oak chairs, which she still had. They have to be the two we worked on, the only ones like them in Greenway.'

LEFT The Hall stand with some of the many hats and walking sticks that were in the Hall.

RIGHT The former Fax Room on the first floor contains a collection of first editions of Agatha Christie novels.

Tessa, who has been a National Trust volunteer here since the beginning, remembers vividly the wonder of her first visit to the house, crammed as it was with possessions – croquet mallets in the hall, umbrella stand stuffed with walking sticks, gardening hats piled on the hall table. It seemed chaotic. Nigel Wollen remembers: 'Greenway was very cluttered in a splendid way. Rosalind's desk was a great slagheap of letters, bills – so spectacular that some artist asked if he could paint it.'

It seemed to Tessa that the left side of Greenway was Agatha's and the right side was the Hicks'.

There were things everywhere – on tables, on shelves, in cupboards, in cabinets. I don't think they threw anything away. Everything higgledy-piggledy – like a treasure trove. Displays of pillboxes, and stamp boxes, watches; walk-in cupboards full of fur coats, evening dress and smock dresses. The saucepans! They never threw a saucepan away. There was pottery that hadn't seen the light of day in years – sometimes you couldn't even see the pattern. And every single book she'd every written was in the house in whatever language – and there were so many.

One particular challenge for the National Trust conservators was the books. It was the first time that the Trust had had to deal with inferior mass-produced paperbacks. Each book had to be assessed and tagged with categories denoting the state of the book,

ABOVE This pair of poreclain magpies and the Meissen mantel clock form part of the collections brought from Ashfield.

OPPOSITE On the wall of the Fax Room is a display of Stevengraphs, machine-embroidered silk pictures pioneered by Thomas Stevens of Coventry, which were collected by all members of the family.

such as a broken spine or torn pages. But what was an almost bigger challenge was the sheer quantity and variety of objects.

'There is no doubt that we were a family of collectors and that I have inherited these attributes,' Agatha wrote in her autobiography. Her parents, she said, had a passion for collecting china – her father loved Meissen. When her grandmother came to live at Ashfield, she brought her collection of Dresden and Capo di Monte with her, and cupboards had to be built to house it. And these, together with the collections of Agatha, Max, Rosalind and Anthony, had all accumulated at Greenway. Some collections were esoteric, some were strangely kitsch. But they provided a common interest, a convivial activity, as different members of the family united in one enthusiasm or another. There were Anthony's botanical plates, Max's Bargeware, Agatha's boxes, Rosalind's watches. Agatha and

Max collected silver, a piece for each year between 1700 and 1800; Anthony and Max were keen on chinoiserie; Agatha and Anthony vied with each other to collect Souvenir ware (wooden or china ornaments with stencilled decorations). Agatha also collected papier-mâché tables, Napoleonic prisoner-of-war straw-work and Tunbridge ware (objects of wood inlaid with mosaics of different-coloured woods).

Richard Lane, who had an antique shop at Torre, remembers Agatha Christie coming in the 1950s to buy Tunbridge ware. 'Her chauffeur came in first and then she came in – she was interested in several items. She was a very big lady – and she drove a very hard bargain. Afterwards, when she'd left, I remember thinking "Hmm, I haven't made much out of that . . ."'

Shortly before Greenway opened to the public for the first time, I went round the house with Mathew, his wife Lucy and three of his colleagues, a tour that was touchingly punctuated by his reminiscences. In the library, Mathew told of how his mother's chair was positioned close to the fist-wide crack that ran from roof to ground, now part of the legend of Greenway. 'Visitors would remark that the crack seemed to be getting wider. "*Non*sense," she would say.' He remembers too 'the lovely deep chair in the corner where my grandmother used to sit and begin her reading for the day, which was voluminous.' The library was Mathew's favourite room: 'it was where, after breakfast, life began.'

He related the story of the plasterwork relief over the fireplace in the housekeeper's room, later used as the winter dining room, representing the story from the Book of Daniel of Shadrach, Meshach and Abednego cast into the fiery furnace by King Nebuchadnezzar but miraculously unscathed: it had once been at Greenway Court but had been tracked down by Max and Anthony during the 1960s in Kingswear, probably taken there by former owner Roope Harris Roope.

In the butler's pantry – soon to be the discovery room and the point where one can take a virtual tour of the house – he

reminisced about Anthony's extensive collection of malt whiskies. And in the inner hall he asked about two tapestries from Abney Hall, 'my birthplace', which, pleasingly, have been discovered to have been made in South Dent, a mere 14 miles (23 kilometres) away from Greenway.

He pointed out 'Master Mathew's bedroom', the narrow bedroom on the top floor with its view over the Dart; the larder 'where my mother used to keep all her tins, some dated 1947'; and the floor-to-ceiling cupboards in the winter dining room: 'See these huge cupboards – into which my mother put *everything*. And the corridor outside to the inner hall was full – just full! Crammed. The shelf here just had vases on it – many, many vases.'

Seeing Greenway in this unfinished state must have been a poignant experience for Mathew, for it was a house full of memories; he had spent large parts of his life here with family and friends. But he was looking forward to the future with hope: 'It was a house full of people, and when people are running through it again, then I will be able to remember it well.'

The intention, for the National Trust and for Mathew, is that Greenway should be a living house once again, with afternoon teas in the kitchen, the letting of a holiday apartment mainly on the top floor and 'fine dining experiences' using the dining room much as Agatha and her family had. As Robyn said, 'The purpose is not just to show Greenway, but to breathe life back into it.'

THE LEGACY –
THE TOURISM AND THE BRAND

'I think people should be interested in books,
and not their authors!'

When Agatha Christie died on 12 January 1976, at the age of eighty-five, lights in two London theatres were dimmed in her honour: at St Martin's, where *The Mousetrap* was in its twenty-fourth year, and at the Savoy, where *The Murder at the Vicarage* was showing. After all, she had been the only playwright to have had three plays running at once in the West End (in 1954: *The Mousetrap*, *Witness for the Prosecution* and *Spider's Web*). *The Mousetrap*, which was developed from a radio drama, *Three Blind Mice* (written at the request of Queen Mary), continues still.

She had planned her gravestone: 'Put on my slate: Sleep after Toyle, Port after Stormie Seas, Ease after Warre, Death after Life, Doth greatly please', lines from Spenser's *Faerie Queene*. She specified the music she wanted: Bach's Air in D from his Third Suite, as well as 'Nimrod' from Elgar's Enigma Variations. These were played, along with the Twenty-third Psalm, 'The Lord is My Shepherd', at the memorial service that was held in May at St Martin-in-the-Fields. There was a reading from Thomas à

Bronze bust of Agatha Christie unveiled in Torquay in 1990, the year of the centenary of her birth.

Kempis, whose book she kept by her bedside, and an address by her publisher, Billy Collins.

After her death, accolades poured in for the best-selling author of all time, though she also had the distinction of being denounced by the Chinese communist press as a 'running dog for the rich and powerful: she described crimes committed by the lower classes of British society, but never explained their social causes' (Alan Coren in *Punch* had fun with that one).

Her last novel, *Sleeping Murder*, featuring Miss Marple and written during the war as an insurance for Max, was published later that year, and *An Autobiography* in 1977. There had been many earlier requests asking for permission to write 'an authorized life' and she had always refused: 'I write books to be sold and I hope people will enjoy them but I think people should be interested in *books* and not their authors!' However, in 1984 Janet Morgan's highly regarded *Agatha Christie: A Biography*, sanctioned by her daughter Rosalind, appeared. Since then there have been books on many aspects of her life – even biographies of Miss Marple and Poirot. In 2005 came the Agatha Project, a computer-aided linguistic study, which allegedly found that her language patterns stimulated higher-than-usual activity in the brain, making her

Sleeping Murder, the last Miss Marple story, was published posthumously in 1976, the year of her death.

books 'literally unputdownable'. And her books continue to be read, appearing in new editions with different covers and attracting fresh audiences. Unlike other best-selling authors whose appeal fades away – indeed Eden Philpotts, Agatha's mentor, is barely remembered now – Agatha Christie remains a strong presence in the publishing world. This is partly because Agatha Christie Ltd was bought by a large corporation that is expert in branding, and also because her daughter Rosalind Hicks and her grandson Mathew Prichard (chairman of Agatha Christie Ltd) worked hard to protect and promote Agatha's work in equal measure.

Occasionally, there were differences of opinion. A letter of apology from Rosalind for her non-attendance at one company AGM points out that

> as a founder-director and my mother's daughter, I do have some strong objections to the current practice of cutting, altering and updating Agatha Christie's words . . . Half the charm of Agatha Christie plays as well as her books is the portrayal of the social customs and style of the period in which it was written . . . [Readers] also like the contemporary details of the time and characters and social behaviour from the 20s to the early 70s, which is why the word 'updating' is abhorrent to me.

While she was not totally opposed to television productions, Rosalind kept a very close eye on them. Of one Alan Plater adaptation she commented: 'Why should Poirot be sent to this hotel for a strict diet of nettle juice? What is the point of the scene in the restaurant anyway? I can't see any point in having Miss Lemon in this story . . .'

Rosalind was always very loyal to her mother's writing, drawing attention once to her 'genius for starting books. Once you've read the opening of *The Body in the Library*, you can't put it down.' On another occasion she declared: 'I am an unashamed fan of my mother's books. I don't know at what age I started reading them, but I can read them over and over again and still find a lot to enjoy in them. She was a great storyteller, and her books are full of humour.'

Those two characteristics may be why her popularity nationally and internationally continues unabated. Back in her home town of Torquay she was not forgotten: in September 1986, for example, the Torbay Civic Society had a birthday memorial excursion to Burgh Island ('Members will have the entire freedom of the island'). There were attempts to capitalize on the associations – though plans for a red-herring-shaped maze outside Torre Abbey were scuppered. But in the following year, the Agatha Christie Memorial Room was opened in Torre Abbey, in what used to be Colonel Cary's study – a wood-panelled room at the end of a staircase and, rather atmospherically, tucked under the clock mechanism. Created by the previous curator, Leslie Retallick, it contained a high-backed armchair, with the 1937 Remington typewriter Agatha used for so many of her novels and the gown she wore when being made Honorary Doctor of Letters at Exeter University. A list made at the time for insurance purposes – with 'tentative values' – shows some of the things in this little room that caught people's imagination:

- Portrait of Agatha Miller by N. Baird.
- Papier mâché fans
- Large straw box
- Small work box
- Shell picture
- Dagger as used in *Murder on the Links*
- Plotting book and corrected manuscript, typed proof and first edition book as issued, *Third Girl*.

When the room was opened in May 1987 Rosalind gave an address, in which she said: 'I am sure my mother would have been pleased and proud to have been honoured in this way by the Torbay Council with a room in the town in which she was born and grew up in and in a county which she always loved.'

There is no trace of Agatha Christie in the newly restored Torre Abbey – though Poirot was the star guest at its reopening: in 2004, David Suchet, who plays Poirot in the television series, had ceremonially locked the door, and in 2008, after a £6 million refurbishment, he unlocked it again. Many of the contents of the Memorial Room have been moved to Greenway, but the link remains, in the new planting of a 'poison garden' in the grounds.

Television adaptations began to be made. Of course, there had been films, which had begun in the 1960s with a series made by MGM starring Margaret Rutherford as Miss Marple. These were not popular with Agatha at all – not least because the stories strayed further and further away from the plots of her books – though she became friendly with Margaret Rutherford and dedicated *The Mirror Crack'd from Side to Side* to her. In 1984 the first of the television adaptations of her Miss Marple stories (*The Body in the Library*) starring Joan Hickson was broadcast. Poirot, played by David Suchet, made his first appearance on television in 1989.

The bandwagon began to roll with the hundredth anniversary celebrations of Agatha Christie's birth in 1990. The first major exhibition of her life was staged at Torquay Museum. There were publications, such as *Agatha Christie: Official Centenary Celebration*, filled with articles on every aspect of her life and works; *A Classic English Crime*, '13 stories for the Christie Centenary by the Crime Writers' Association', published in her honour; souvenir editions of the local paper, the *Herald Express*. The Agatha Christie Mile, a trail visiting landmarks of Agatha's life in Torquay, was inaugurated. A bronze bust sculpted by Dutch artist Carol Van den Boom-Cairns was unveiled by Rosalind in Cary Green – appropriately outside the tourist information office and what is now the English Riviera shop, which is filled with

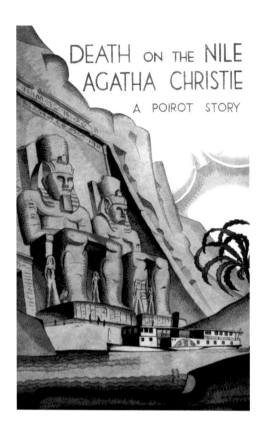

FAR LEFT *Death on the Nile* is one of the group of the best-known Agatha Christie books, which provide inspiration for the many artefacts on sale in the English Riviera shop.

LEFT One of the plaques that mark the Agatha Christie Mile in Torquay.

RIGHT Torquay Harbour, site of the Regatta that enthralled Agatha as a young girl and which still takes place every August.

Agatha Christie books, CDs, DVDs as well as canvas book bags (imprinted with *Destination Unknown* and *4.50 from Paddington*), tea towels (*Labours of Hercules*) and jigsaw puzzles of *The Body in the Library* and *Death on the Nile*: it is Agatha Christie nirvana.

And on the centenary weekend itself, matters reached fever pitch. Sue Arnold, reporting for the *Observer*, gave a flavour of the international frenzy over the anniversary by recounting the experiences of the hotels most associated with Agatha: at the Imperial, 'upon whose terrace Miss Marple explained who did it and how in *Sleeping Murder* . . . the manager was telling an Australian journalist about the first world Cluedo championships being held in the ballroom (or was it the conservatory with the piece of lead pipe?) while the assistant manager of The Grand spent an entire morning being interviewed by Japanese television . . . [who] wanted to know why the first lady of detection spent her honeymoon in Torquay if she lived there.' The Orient Express arrived in town from Victoria station in London, full of tourist board officials and actors and actresses. David Suchet and Joan Hickson met on the platform at Torquay station as Poirot and Miss Marple never had in life.

The centrepiece of the celebrations was the Agatha Christie centenary banquet at the English Riviera Centre on Saturday, 15 September 1990, exactly a hundred years after her birth. The menu was avowedly local: Dart salmon mousse, Devonshire beef, Dartmoor autumn fruit salad with clotted cream. The forty-one tables were named after her books: suitably, the top table was labelled *The Mysterious Affair at Styles,* as that was the book that started it all. Nigel Wollen, the family solicitor, was on *The Body in the Library*; George Gowler, one-time butler at Greenway, was on *Dead Man's Folly*, which was set at Greenway. Peter Mallowan, a nephew of Max Mallowan, was on *Murder in Mesopotamia.*

Three years later, in 1993, the Agatha Christie Society was formed 'to promote communications between the many and loyal fans of Agatha Christie and the various media who strive to bring her works in their various forms to the public'. After a year, the society had nearly four hundred members and was 'proud to have its first gathering in Torquay to coincide with the Mystery on the English Riviera Festival'. The Celebration of Mystery Fiction in 1994 featured a tea dance, a Murder Evening at the Weary Ploughman by Churston station and a competition staged by Torquay Museum called '10 ways to Kill the Curator'. In a crowning touch, Rosalind Hicks opened Greenway for society members who, as the *Herald Express* somewhat inaccurately reported, 'were enthralled with the rare opportunity to stand in the room where Dame Agatha wrote her books and to wander in the beautiful gardens which inspired so much of her writing'.

Tourists on the crime writer's trail began to arrive in Torquay in greater numbers. Joan Nott has met many of them. A Blue Badge guide for over thirty years and 2005 winner of an English Riviera award for services to tourism, she had begun, with her late husband Michael, to develop her expertise in Agatha Christie's life and works in the 1980s. (It is thanks to their efforts in trawling through the Exeter University archives that Agatha's baptismal record is on the wall at All Saints' Church.) 'I was really the first person to start researching her roots in Torquay. Until then no one had pulled those strands together.'

The first Agatha Christie tour Joan led was for the Murder Mystery Book Club of San Diego in California. Since then she has conducted such tours for people from all over the world and has a fat file of appreciative letters from the Philippines, France, Holland, America, Australia, Sweden. Not long ago, she showed round a Chinese film producer in her twenties. 'Her mother read her Agatha Christie novels as bedtime stories – while children here were being read Peter Rabbit!' So fascinated had she been by this childhood experience that she came back to make a film

about Agatha Christie's home town. In the 2008 Agatha Christie Festival walk Joan had among others a Dutch couple, six Filipinos who had come down from London and a German couple – 'of course, they like Margaret Rutherford'.

Agatha Christie Week was inaugurated in 2005 on the seventy-fifth anniversary of the first Miss Marple novel, *The Murder at the Vicarage*, to mark the life and times of the author nationally, and to take place each September around her birthday. That year, Torquay staged its first festival as part of it – a relatively modest affair with a Murder Mystery tour, events and an exhibition at the Torquay Museum, visits to Greenway's gardens and performances of *A Murder is Announced* and *The Unexpected Guest*. This was the year when the Agatha Christie Theatre Company was set up through a partnership between Agatha Christie Ltd and West End producer Bill Kenwright, with exclusive rights to adapt her work for touring productions.

In the following years, the festival gathered steam, with plays staged by the Agatha Christie Company at the Princess Theatre, open-air screenings of films, and 'sea and river voyages' to Greenway, until in 2008 there was a programme of dozens of events, from cream tea at the Grand Hotel to a classic car treasure hunt. The Torquay Museum with its exhibition and shop – the best place for second-hand copies and first editions – plays a central part in the festival, and was the venue for the newsworthy coup of 2008: the first airing by Mathew Prichard of extracts from thirteen and a half hours of tapes discovered at Greenway in a cardboard box and brought back to life by Eurion Brown, a specialist near Mathew's home in Glamorgan. The recording turned out to be part of Agatha's autobiography read by her, with many clicks of the on/off switch, into a Grundig Memorette. The broadcast to the packed audience had the air of being rather an event (the voice of Agatha Christie – notoriously reluctant to give interviews or make public appearances – was heard on BBC Radio 4's *Today* programme that week as a result of the discovery). Mathew Prichard announced that evening: 'It is a piece of history in some way. Hopefully it is helping you to learn more about the person behind the voice . . . she was modest, with a great sense of humour.' He pointed out the distinctive flavour of these tapes: 'She is talking to nobody here and that is why she has such confidence in herself and becomes almost lyrical about certain subjects.'

The festival also featured the traditional treats of a Murder Mystery Dinner, starring the Murder Made to Measure theatre group, and a Tea Dance, complete with Devon cream teas and a game of Poirot Investigates (a version of Wink Murder) on each table. This was held at Oldway Mansion, the glittering edifice built in 1874 for Isaac Singer, the sewing-machine manufacturer, and visited by Agatha Christie. Setting the tone on the day, parked outside were the vintage cars of Torbay Old Wheelers in which some of the guests had arrived. The mansion is a glorious building in French Renaissance style, with an extravagantly decorated entrance hall and staircase dominated by a huge painting of the coronation of Josephine by the Emperor Napoleon (a copy of David's original). The ballroom with its sprung floor and gilt-edged mirrors is a perfect venue for a tea dance.

At the 2008 event, a sell-out, guests entered into the spirit of the thing, dressing in boas, feathered headbands, pearl chokers, cloche hats, white gloves and sequinned garments. Some perfectionism was in evidence, with assessments of the appropriateness of the garments – 'that pink flowery dress with silver belt is much more the thing,' said one critical bystander. 'After all, this is an *afternoon* dance.' Dancing was to the music of the High Society Band, who played such hardy perennials as 'April Showers' and 'My Blue Heaven'. The guests showed themselves to be proficient dancers, from the rather portly man who, carrying his stomach before him, was remarkably light on his feet, to the couple who, as the afternoon wore on, drew all eyes – especially when demonstrating the Charleston, two-tone shoes twinkling in perfect unison. Henry Eisner and Mary Jennings turned out to be leading lights in the

Oldway Mansion in Paignton, built by Isaac Singer, the sewing machine millionaire, where Agatha Christie attended dances in the fine ballroom.

San Diego Vintage Dance Society. They were not the only overseas visitors: others had come from South Africa, Canada and Japan.

The Japanese are particularly interested in Agatha Christie. Shortly before Agatha Christie Week, Professor Watanabe from Tokyo had given a lecture at the Torquay Museum on the cultural interest of Japanese people in her. He had been an ardent fan of her books since the 1970s, and finally visited Torquay in 2000.

Agatha Christie Week is put together by a committee in Torquay working in close conjunction with Agatha Christie Ltd, conscious always of the need to protect and promote. The promotion and branding is not new. When *A Murder is Announced* was published in 1950, it was Agatha's fiftieth book, so 50,000 were printed (and it was honoured by a Foyles Literary Luncheon at the Dorchester). It was no coincidence that, with slightly creative counting, her eightieth book was produced for her eightieth birthday. The slogan 'A Christie for Christmas' was coined. Despite her reticence and her unwillingness to speak in public, Agatha Christie was a professional to the last and understood the value of such things.

Under the guidance of her grandson, Mathew Prichard, the brand continues. In 1998, Agatha Christie Ltd became part of Chorion with its expertise in global franchising and which owns the rights of a multitude of characters from the Mr Men to the Famous Five and the literary estates of several authors from Raymond Chandler to George Simenon. The official Agatha Christie website, launched soon afterwards, shows Christiean levels of ingenuity in tapping into the continuing interest in Agatha Christie, with games, interactive sections, news and information about events and adaptations. The former Agatha Christie Society was subsumed into the forum of the official website, where fans can communicate with each other. Contributors to the website from Belarus and Bulgaria to India and Argentina discuss titles, characters, and the life of Agatha Christie: one fan said: 'I will be visiting her house and I feel quite emotional about it, to be in the rooms where she lived and feel the atmosphere. I have been a huge fan for more than 25 years and she made me the Devon-lover I have become.' Many other websites and groups pay homage. Her books continue to sell in their millions, and the enthusiasm for her work continues to grow in all parts of the world.

But her most personal legacy is at Greenway. Here visitors can see the brass-bound chest, which was the hiding-place for a body in 'The Mystery of the Baghdad Chest', pictures of Mathew and his family on a table in the inner hall, the Greenway editions on the shelf near the window in the library. In the morning room, returned from the green of Rosalind's era to the light colours favoured by Agatha, they can look at the portrait of Agatha as a child and the shell collages she collected. In the drawing room they can inspect the comfortable chairs and sofas from Ashfield, her father's Meissen collection, Agatha's writing desk – and can sometimes hear music from her grand piano, played by volunteers. They may hear too recorded reminiscences on tapes secreted in old Roberts radios – from Mathew in the library talking about the frieze, and from Agatha herself in the drawing room, talking about her working methods.

Not on view is the bath that Agatha took such care over selecting, though the bathroom on the top floor, in the holiday apartment, sports one of a similar design. But her bedroom is. It has been 'conserved, not restored', the walls still painted the colour of cream she chose. Here is her bed, with Max's little bed by the wall. Between the windows, with their sweeping views over the Dart, is the Damascus chest of drawers, inlaid with mother-of-pearl and silver, which, as she recounts in her autobiography, gave her sleepless nights when the wood inside was being eaten by a worm. On the shelves next to the mantelpiece she herself painted are the books she read, from volumes on Devon to novels by other crime writers. In the dressing room are glimpses of the evening dresses and coats she left there. On the outside of the door are still the scratch marks left by a dog trying to get in. It is an enthralling glimpse into a very private person.

On the first day Greenway was open to the public, over four hundred visitors came to see the private home of the public figure. In the first group shown round was a woman who was in a state of elation. She had been the very first person to pre-book her car in, she said. She had waited so long for this moment. She had been determined to be there on the first day, and there she was in the first group of people to see the house. It was a highlight of her life.

'What I wish most for Greenway,' said Mathew, 'is that people who visit it feel some of the magic and sense of place that I felt when my family and I spent so much time there in the 1950s and 1960s.' The work of Agatha Christie has entertained and even brought comfort to millions of readers. Now at Greenway her followers can gain further insight into Devon, the place that brought her happiness and inspiration, as well as the home that was so important to her and the vibrant, energetic and exuberant personality of this most private of individuals, the Queen of Crime.

Hanging in one of the bedrooms of the holiday apartment at Greenway are portraits of Agatha's parents, Clara and Frederick Miller.

SELECT BIBLIOGRAPHY

Christie, Agatha, *An Autobiography* (Collins, 1977)
Christie, Agatha (all published by Collins and Penguin):
  The Mysterious Affair at Styles (1920)
  The Man in the Brown Suit (1924)
  The Secret of Chimneys (1925)
  The Murder of Roger Ackroyd (1926)
  The Mystery of the Blue Train (1928)
  The Murder at the Vicarage (1930)
  The Sittaford Mystery (1931)
  Peril at End House (1932)
  Murder on the Orient Express (1934)
  Why Didn't They Ask Evans? (1934)
  Parker Pyne Investigates (1934)
  Three Act Tragedy (1935)
  The ABC Murders (1936)
  Dumb Witness (1937)
  Ten Little Niggers (*And Then There Were None*) (1939)
  The Regatta Mystery (short stories) (1939)
  Sad Cypress (1940)
  One, Two, Buckle My Shoe (1940)
  Evil Under the Sun (1941)
  N or M? (1941)
  The Body in the Library (1942)
  Five Little Pigs (1942)
  The Moving Finger (1943)
  Towards Zero (1944)
  The Hollow (1946)
  Taken at the Flood (1948)
  Mrs McGinty's Dead (1952)
  After the Funeral (1953)
  A Pocket Full of Rye (1953)
  Dead Man's Folly (1956)
  4.50 from Paddington (1957)
  Ordeal by Innocence (1958)
  The Adventure of the Christmas Pudding (short stories) (1960)
  The Pale Horse (1961)
  The Clocks (1963)
  Endless Night (1967)
  Passenger to Frankfurt (1970)
  Nemesis (1971)
  Postern of Fate (1973)
  Curtain (1975)
  Sleeping Murder (1976)
  Miss Marple's Final Cases (1979)
Christie, Agatha, as Mary Westmacott:
  Giant's Bread (1930)
  Unfinished Portrait (1934)
  Absent in the Spring (1944)
  The Rose and the Yew Tree (1948)
Gerrard, David, *Exploring Agatha Christie* Country (Agatha Christie Ltd and English Riviera Tourist Board, 1996)
Hart, Anne, *Agatha Christie's Marple: The Life and Times of Miss Jane Marple* (Collins, 1997)
Hart, Anne, *Poirot: The Life and Times of Hercule Poirot* (Collins, 1997)
Mallowan Christie, Agatha, *Come, Tell Me How You Live* (Collins, 1946)
Mallowan, Max, *Mallowan's Memoirs: Agatha and the Archaeologist* (Collins, 1977)
McCall Henrietta, *The Life of Max Mallowan: Archaeology and Agatha Christie* (British Museum Press, 2001)
Morgan, Janet, *Agatha Christie: A Biography* (Collins, 1984)
Osborne, Charles, *The Life and Crime of Agatha Christie* (Collins, 1999)
Porter, Tony, *The Great White Palace* (Deerhill Books, 2005)
Risdon, John, *The River Dart* (Halsgrove, 2004)
Rowse A.L., *Memories and Glimpses* (Methuen, 1986)
Saunders, Peter, *The Mousetrap Man* (Collins, 1972)
Sobel, Dava, *Agatha Christie A to Z* (Checkmark Books, 1996)
Symons, Julian, *Bloody Murder* (Pan Books, 1994)
Thompson, Laura, *Agatha Christie: An English Mystery* (Headline, 2007)
Tregaskes, Jean, *Churston Story, 1088–1998* (Westcountry Studies Library, 1998)
Wagstaff, Vanessa and Poole, Stephen, *Agatha Christie: A Reader's Companion* (Aurum, 2004)
Williams, W, *Allen Lane: A Personal Portrait* (The Bodley Head, 1973)

FURTHER INFORMATION

PLACES TO VISIT

Greenway, Greenway Road, Galmpton, nr Brixham, Devon
TQ5 0ES; tel: 01803 842382 www.nationaltrust.org.uk
Visitors arriving by car must book in advance. See below for
river transport.

For holiday accommodation, contact National Trust Cottages,
PO Box 536, Melksham, Wiltshire SN12 8SX; tel: 0844 800
2070; www.nationaltrustcottages.co.uk

Torquay Museum, 529 Babbacombe Road, Torquay TQ1 1HG;
tel: 01803 293975; www.torquaymuseum.org

Torre Abbey, The King's Drive, Torquay TQ2 5JE;
tel: 01803 293593; www.torre-abbey.org.uk

Cockington Village, Torquay TQ2 6XA; tel: 01803 606035;
www.countryside-trust.org.uk

Kents Cavern, Ilsham Road, Torquay TQ1 2JF; tel: 01803 215136;
www.kents-cavern.co.uk

Oldway Mansion, Paignton TQ3 2TD; tel: 01803 207933

Dartington Hall, Totnes, South Devon TQ9 6EL;
tel: 01803 847147; www.dartingtonhall.com

HOTELS

The Grand Hotel, Seafront, Torquay TQ2 6NT tel: 0800 44 888 44.
www.grandtorquay.co.uk

The Imperial, Park Hill Road, Torquay TQ1 2DG; tel: 01803
294301; www.barcelo-hotels.co.uk

Corbyn Head Hotel, Torbay Road, Seafront, Torquay TQ2 6RH;
tel: 01803 213611; www.corbynhead.com
(with award-winning Orchid Restaurant)

Burgh Island Hotel, Bigbury-on-Sea, TQ7 4BG; tel: 01548 810514;
www.burghisland.com

Manor Inn, 2 Stoke Gabriel Road, Galmpton TQ5 0NL;
tel: 01803 661101; www.manorinngalmpton.co.uk

For enquiries about Moorlands, contact HF Holidays;
tel: 0845 470 7558; www.hf-holidays.co.uk

TRANSPORT

Paignton and Dartmouth Steam Railway, tel: 01803 555872;
www.paignton-steamrailway.co.uk

South Devon Railway, The Station, Buckfastleigh, TQ11 0DZ;
tel: 0845 345 1420; www.southdevonrailway.org

Greenway Quay and Ferry Service provides trips from Dartmouth
and Torquay to Greenway: tel: 01803 844010;
www.greenwayferry.co.uk

Dartmouth–Dittisham Ferry: tel: 0781 800 1108;
www.dartmouthdittishamferry.co.uk

River Link (for Dart cruises and Round Robin on steam railway and
ferry): Dart Pleasure Craft, 5 Lower Street, Dartmouth TQ6 9AJ;
tel: 01803 834488; www.riverlink.co.uk

OTHER USEFUL WEBSITES

www.agathachristie.com

www.torquay.com

www.torbytes.co.uk

www.galmptontorbay.org.uk

www.dittisham.org.uk

www.library.exeter.ac.uk/special

TOURIST INFORMATION

English Riviera Tourist Board, 5 Vaughan Parade, Torquay TQ2 5JG;
tel: 01803 211211; www.englishriviera.co.uk

Visit South Devon (South Hams and Teignbridge Tourism),
Lower Tweed Mill, Shinners Bridge, Dartington, Totnes TQ9 6JB;
tel: 01803 847502; www.visitsouthdevon.co.uk

Dartmoor National Park Authority, Parke, Bovey Tracey TQ13 9JQ;
tel: 01626 832093; www.dartmoor-npa.gov.uk

Haytor Information Centre, on B3387, three miles west of
Bovey Tracey tel: 01364 661520

Dartmouth Tourist Information, The Engine House, Mayors
Avenue, Dartmouth TQ6 9YY; tel: 01803 834224; www.
discoverdartmouth.com

Salcombe Tourist Information, Market Street, Salcombe TQ8 8DE;
tel: 01548 843927; www.salcombeinformation.co.uk

Agatha Christie Week is held every September. More information
on events in Torquay from www.englishriviera.co.uk and on events
round the country from www.agathachristie.com

INDEX

Page numbers in *italics* refer to illustrations

ACKNOWLEDGMENTS

AUTHOR'S ACKNOWLEDGMENTS

I want to thank many people and organizations for their part in making the process of researching and writing this book so enjoyable: primarily, Mathew Prichard, not only for his encouragement and invaluable provision of material but also for his generosity and good company, and also his wife Lucy for her kind hospitality. Thank you too to others at Agatha Christie Ltd, including Joanne Fowler, Tamsen Harward and Jemma Jones. Also crucial to the success of this enterprise was the help given by the National Trust generally, and specifically Claire Bolitho, Maggie Bush – and especially Robyn Brown for sparing time to talk to me amid the busiest period of the restoration of Greenway. I could not have managed without the assistance of the English Riviera Tourist Board, who first invited me to Torquay in 2005 to write about Agatha Christie's birthplace and home, an enlightening visit organized by Ian Weightman: many members of staff have been most supportive, including Georgina Bowen and Lydia Stone, but I would particularly like to mention George Brewer, who has been constantly and cheerfully helpful.

I'd also like to thank Ros Palmer and Geoff Old of Torquay Museum, Katie Lusty of Torquay Library Services, Christine Faunch of Exeter University Library and Yvonne Widger of Dartington Hall, all of whom provided access to their collections and generous assistance with last-minute queries. Polly Birchall and Sarah Streeter of Visit South Devon gave valuable help with pictures. Martin Yates provided an elusive piece of information about Penguins. Barry Edwards lent me two books that led to a pleasurable encounter.

I very much enjoyed meeting: Nigel Wollen for his memories of the Miller/Christie family and Greenway; Joan Nott, for sharing her considerable knowledge about Agatha Christie; Tessa Tattersall for her insights into Greenway; John Risdon for talking of his love of the Dart and Galmpton area; Bob Bowling for helping unravel a mystery at Churston church; Keith Clarke, who told me about Moorlands; Tony and B Porter for stories about Burgh Island.

I am very grateful to all at Frances Lincoln: John Nicoll for accepting and broadening my original idea; Andrew Dunn, who has worked with it enthusiastically; Anne Askwith for being a sympathetic and discerning editor; Becky Clarke, who designed the book; and Sarah Mitchell, proofreader. Particular thanks to Emma O'Bryen, who suggested I propose the book in first place.

Finally, I would like to thank Anna and Judith Shipman for their encouragement and advice, but, above all, Michael Shipman, who has accompanied me on many trips to Devon, taken lovely photographs for me, read my text and now knows a great deal about Agatha Christie.

PICTURE CREDITS

TEXT ACKNOWLEDGMENTS